The History of Camp Tracy

Japanese WWII POWs and the Future of Strategic Interrogation

Alexander D. Corbin

Ziedon Press

Published by Ziedon Press, Fort Belvoir, VA 22060

THE HISTORY OF CAMP TRACY: JAPANESE WWII POWS AND
THE FUTURE OF STRATEGIC INTERROGATION

ISBN-13: 978-0-578-02979-5
Library of Congress Control Number: 2009931343

Maps by Marcy Protteau
Printed in the United States of America

The views expressed in this book are those of the author and do not reflect
the official policy or position of the Department of Defense or the U.S.
Government.

To order additional copies of this book please visit:
http://stores.lulu.com/ziedon_press

To the U.S. Army and Navy interrogators of Camp Tracy, more of whom are lost every day due to the passage of time. Their diligent efforts and selfless service during World War II continue to guide and inform us today and truly distinguish them as the Greatest Generation.

To my wife, Leilani; she is the source of all my strength, and makes me a better person for just being around her. It is due to her continued dedication and support that this book came into being.

Camp Sa
Fort Sne

University of Colorado,

Angel Island, CA
Camp Stoneman, CA
Camp Tracy, CA

PACIFIC
OCEAN

125°W   120°W   115°W   110°W   105°W   100°W

70°N

60°N

Bering
Sea

Gulf of Alaska

km 0 250 500

mi 0   250   500

50°N   160°W   140°W

160°W   156°W

22°N

20°N

km 0 100 200

mi 0   100   200

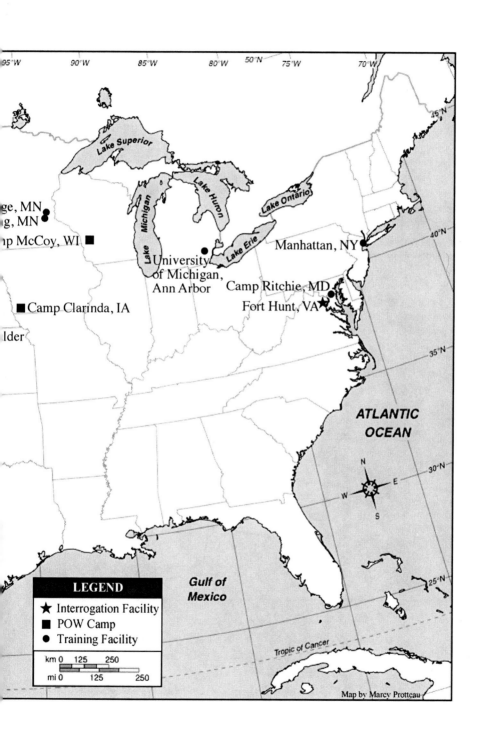

95°W   90°W   85°W   80°W   50°N   75°W   70°W

45°N

Lake Superior

40°N

ge, MN
g, MN
p McCoy, WI ■

Lake Michigan   Lake Huron
Lake Ontario
University
of Michigan,
Ann Arbor   Lake Erie
Manhattan, NY

■ Camp Clarinda, IA
Camp Ritchie, MD
Fort Hunt, VA

lder

35°N

ATLANTIC
OCEAN

30°N

N
W   E
S

Gulf of
Mexico

25°N

LEGEND
★ Interrogation Facility
■ POW Camp
● Training Facility

km 0   125   250
mi 0   125   250

Tropic of Cancer

Map by Marcy Protteau

Camp Tracy

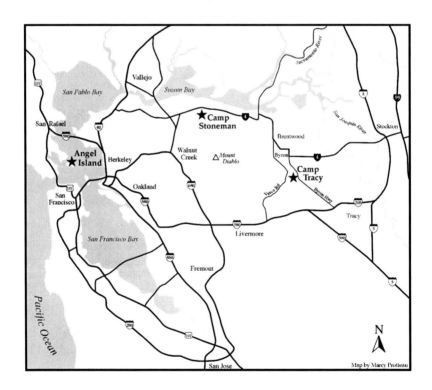

Map by Marcy Protteau

Contents

Foreword

O n October 5th and 6th, 2007, the veterans of "P.O. Box 1142," code name for a World War II top secret strategic interrogation facility located at Fort Hunt, Virginia, ten miles south of Washington, DC, were able finally to break their sixty-year silence. In a first-of-its-kind, two-day reunion and symposium sponsored by the National Park Service, former U.S. Army and Navy interrogators, now in their 80s and 90s, met to receive formal government recognition for their critical contributions in defeating Nazi Germany, to renew past friendships, and to commiserate about interrogation techniques then and now. Among the more than 4,000 prisoners of war (POWs) who were hosted temporarily at Fort Hunt from 1941 to 1946, most were captured German submariners, scientists and engineers, and senior military officers.[1] According to David Vela, superintendent of the George Washington Memorial Parkway (who now oversees the property where Fort Hunt once stood), "What these men did led to both winning the war and the peace that followed."[2]   The information gleaned from their interrogations provided the technical foundation on which the United States built its eventual strategic success in the Cold War. To these aging veterans, many of whom were immigrant Jews who had fled Europe to escape Nazi persecution, of equal importance to their accomplishments was how they conducted themselves when dealing with prisoners who represented a system they loathed. George Frenkel, 87, of Kensington, Maryland explained that "during the many interrogations I never laid hands on anyone.... We extracted information in a battle of wits. I'm proud to say I never compromised my humanity."[3]

Among those invited to attend the P.O. Box 1142 symposium was U.S. Army Major Alexander D. Corbin, then my student at the National Defense Intelligence College. At the time, Alex was just beginning his research for a master's thesis dealing with Fort Hunt's similarly secretive sister facility, Camp Tracy, California, set up at about the same time to conduct strategic interrogation primarily of Japanese POWs. Captivated by the Fort Hunt veterans and their achievements, and introduced at the symposium to potential resources available at the National Archives and Records Administration, Alex resolved to tell the equally compelling story of Camp Tracy. But his resulting thesis and now book, winner of the Joint History Office's Fleet Admiral Chester W. Nimitz Archival Research Award for 2008, is much more than just a historical narrative of events long past. Alex served at Forward Operating Base Abu Ghraib, Iraq during Operation IRAQI FREEDOM— arriving there in January 2004, shortly before the revelations of the Abu Ghraib prisoner abuses shocked the world in April 2004. In their aftermath, Alex's military intelligence unit was tasked with rebuilding prisoner handling procedures, reinstituting appropriate training, and reestablishing interrogation oversight to ensure such abuses would never be repeated. With this experience fresh in his mind, Alex came to the National Defense Intelligence College determined to find better ways of eliciting information from prisoners captured in the Global War on Terror. He sought his answers by examining the following question: *What lessons can be learned from the experience of Camp Tracy, a U.S. strategic interrogation center for Japanese prisoners of war during World War II, which can influence existing and future U.S. interrogation policies, doctrine, and practices?*

Recalling the atmosphere of fear and uncertainty that gripped the country and the administration immediately following the 9/11 attacks, President George W. Bush explained in 2006 that the United States, in "respond[ing] to the attack on our country…had to wage an unprecedented war against an enemy *unlike any we had fought before.*"[4] But in reality, Alex's research suggests, this new Islamic extremist enemy is not so different from enemies the United States had previously encountered. During World War II, the United States fought and won a war against another implacable foe, the Japanese Empire, whose combatants, even more numerous and threatening than today's Islamic extremists, formed an equally self-sacrificial, religiously motivated warrior-class profoundly alien to most Americans in culture, language, appearance, and religion.

Prior to his assignment at Abu Ghraib, Alex already had extensive interrogation experience. As an U.S. Army trained Arabic interrogator, and with undergraduate work in Middle East Studies, Alex had developed a sophisticated understanding of Arab and

Islamic cultures. However, to understand the parallels between Japanese extremists and Islamic extremists, Alex had to immerse himself in the unique aspects of Japanese history, culture, and mindset. A meticulous researcher, Alex consulted relevant accounts published before the beginning of World War II, as well as contemporary authors; one author even provided Alex with personal research notes he had taken while translating Japanese POWs' memoirs into English. The primary basis for Alex's research was declassified archival documents, many of which had not seen the light of day in over sixty years. In the process he uncovered personnel rosters of U.S. Army and Navy interrogators stationed at Camp Tracy during World War II. Though almost all are now deceased, Alex succeeded in tracking down and interviewing seven Camp Tracy veterans. Most of these men, now in their 80s or 90s, had never spoken publicly of their involvement with Camp Tracy until Alex contacted them.

While other books have touched on interrogations of Japanese POWs during World War II, especially the role of the Nisei (literally second generation, denoting the first native-born Americans from Japanese immigrant parents), none have related these activities to detailed operations of wartime Joint Interrogation Centers (JICs). Today, as Alex notes, the mere mention of detention and interrogation centers customarily evokes two images: the first is the scandalous and indecent treatment of detainees at the Abu Ghraib prison in Iraq; and the second is the allegation of torture and abuse of detainees held at the U.S. Naval Base in Guantanamo Bay, Cuba. Alex's personal experience at Abu Ghraib prison and his study of JIC operations at Camp Tracy have convinced him of several important conclusions relevant for interrogation activities being conducted now, some sixty-five years later, and in the future. Among those conclusions:

- The strict adherence to the security and secrecy that cloaked Camp Tracy provided POWs with the relative assurance that the information they disclosed—in effect betrayals of their country—would remain private and that the POWs would not suffer any additional dishonor or disgrace.
- The stringent pre-screening of POWs assured that only those POWs who possessed strategic-level information were sent to Camp Tracy. This pre-screening further allowed interrogators to devote more time and effort to tailoring approaches to individual POWs.
- The use of interrogator teams, consisting of a Caucasian and a Nisei, combined the cultural awareness of the Caucasian interrogators, and the Japanese heritage and physical racial characteristics of the Nisei, into one highly successful interrogation package.
- The use of torture or "physical coercion" was not necessary; in fact the opposite was true: Camp Tracy interrogators found that courtesy and kindness overcame most Japanese reluctance and reticence.

Alex's findings have direct bearing on the U.S. military's ability to achieve success in its current and future interrogation operations in the Global War on Terror. By examining Camp Tracy's Joint Interrogation Center operations in detail, Alex was able to highlight the policies, doctrine, and practices used effectively in carrying out interrogation operations during World War II, which can readily be applied to the GWOT. Major Corbin's book is a clear winner. Its contributions serve as an outstanding example of the benefits of archival research to the intelligence enterprise. Air Force Colonel Steven Kleinman, a highly experienced interrogator and national commentator on interrogation activities, described, in a letter to Alex Corbin, the transformational value of Alex's research: "I will be testifying on detainee and interrogation policies before Congressional committees...and will also be participating in a senior panel convened to design a way ahead on interrogation for the next administration. I cannot think of a higher compliment to pay you than to assure you that I will refer to your thesis in making my arguments."[5]

John A. Wahlquist
Colonel, USAF (Ret)
Faculty Member
National Defense Intelligence College
November 5, 2008

Preface

O ne of the issues I wrestled with while I was writing this book was conveying as accurately as possible the hatred, mistrust, and animosity that existed between Americans and Japanese during World War II (WWII). That era was a dark time in U.S. history, when exceptionally high levels of suspicion and fear led the U.S. government to round up Japanese-American citizens and lock them away in internment camps, while the Supreme Court set a precedent by stripping away their civil rights. However, this animosity was not just one-sided; the Japanese similarly displayed a great level of distrust and hatred towards Americans. This mutual hatred led to some of the bloodiest battles of WWII, and perhaps of all modern times.

To remain true to the negative sentiments of that historical period, and to portray them accurately, I have not softened the language Americans used to describe the Japanese, nor the common

Japanese perceptions of Americans. This is not to say that all Americans felt this way, nor that all Japanese felt this way either. My intent is to capture and relate the common sentiments and perceptions of the time. While some readers might question my decision and take offense at the harsh words that appear in my account, I feel that those words are important for a full understanding of the environment of the time. This faithfulness to what was actually said and felt further highlights the important wartime-role that Japanese-Americans—even as their families were isolated in internment camps—played in gathering intelligence. We can learn much from the selfless service and sacrifice of these Americans, and apply those lessons to the world we live in today.

-ADC

Acknowledgments

I began working on this project in the fall of 2007, spending months digging through dusty records and tracking down Camp Tracy veterans. During my quest, I was guided by my advisors, John A. Wahlquist and Steven M. Kleinman, to both of whom I am greatly indebted. I would also like to thank Brandon Bies of the U.S. National Park Service, Carol Jensen of the East Contra Costa Historical Society, Rick Straus, Cartographer Marcy Protteau, Photographer Kim Romena, my personal editor Denise de la Cruz, the Japanese-American Veterans Association (JAVA), the Military Intelligence Service (MIS) Veterans Association and most importantly all of the U.S. Army and Navy veterans who were willing to take a few hours of their time to share with me their experiences at Camp Tracy.

Finally, I acknowledge the unflagging support, advice, and encouragement of my wife, Leilani, to whom this work is dedicated.

Chapter 1

Echoes From the Past

Learn from our successes and mistakes to anticipate and be ready for new challenges.
—The National Intelligence Strategy of the United States of America, 2005[1]

The United States Global War on Terrorism (GWOT) is in its sixth year with no end in sight. Intelligence gathering is crucial in the successful prosecution of this struggle as evidenced by Vice Chairman of the U.S. Senate Select Committee on Intelligence Senator Christopher "Kit" Bond's remarks on the Senate floor during a debate on the 2007 Intelligence Authorization Act: "intelligence is so important in this global war on terror declared on us by al-Qaida and radical Islamists—not a war we started but a war they started, that can only be countered by good intelligence."[2] Towards this endeavor, on July 20, 2007, President George W. Bush issued an Executive Order justifying the detention and interrogation of unlawful enemy combatants. President Bush, during a press conference at the White House, defended his decision:

> I have put this program in place for a reason, and that is to better protect the American people, and when we find somebody who may have information regarding a potential attack on America, you bet we're going to detain them, and you bet we're going to question them, because the American people expect us to find out information—actionable intelligence so we can help protect them. That's our job.[3]

Recently however, the mere mentioning of detention and interrogation usually evokes two images. The first is of the scandalous and now infamous treatment of detainees, by U.S. service members, at the Abu Ghraib prison in Iraq. The second is of Camp Delta, the detainment facility at Guantanamo Bay in Cuba—commonly known as GITMO—awash with allegations of torture and reports of *Quran* desecration. These images have weakened U.S. credibility across the globe, and strengthened both the will of the terrorists and their ranks.[4]

Concerning interrogation operations, the United States cannot afford to lose further credibility within the international community. However, to successfully prosecute the GWOT, the United States still requires actionable intelligence to thwart its enemies and protect its national security. The dilemma lies in determining how the United States can successfully obtain the requisite information from a foreign and hostile enemy while abiding by the law and avoiding further alienating the international community.

Fortunately, the GWOT is not the first time the United States has fought a war against a people that were profoundly different from Americans in culture, appearance, and religion. This foe spoke an entirely different language, including an alien-looking written script, all of which were incomprehensible to the average American. This foe was physically different from the average American; shorter, darker with distinctive facial features that led some Americans to view them as "jaundiced baboons," or "monkey-men."[5] This foe believed its leader was a divine being, whose cult of personality was inculcated into each of them from the earliest age. It was this ardent belief in their leader that inspired this foe to carry out suicidal attacks against American forces with fervent and fanatical zeal. The foe was Japan and the war was, of course, World War II (WWII). There are many parallels that can be drawn between the Islamic radicals the United States fights today and the average Japanese soldier during WWII.

To gain the intelligence necessary to combat the Japanese, the United States established a highly secretive strategic-level Joint Interrogation Center at Byron Hot Springs, California, known as Camp Tracy, for the purpose of interrogating Japanese prisoners of war (POWs). The U.S. Army and U.S. Navy combed through their ranks to select well-educated and highly trained interrogators, versed in Japanese culture and knowledgeable of the Japanese language, to operate the Joint Interrogation Center. These personnel established interrogation procedures and developed interrogation techniques that, during the course of Camp Tracy's existence from January 1943 to July 1945, resulted in nearly 12,000 successful interrogations of over 3,500 Japanese POWs.[6]

By looking back at how the United States conducted interrogations against the Japanese, valuable lessons can be distilled and applied for prosecuting the GWOT both today and in the future.

The majority of information in this book is comprised of declassified WWII-era archival documents held at the National Archives and Records Administration (NARA) in College Park, Maryland. Over the past ten years, thousands of previously classified governmental records from the WWII-era have been declassified and made available to the public. This book benefits from original WWII documentation as a direct result of these declassifications, to include: War Department official memoranda, interrogation planning and policy documents, POW interrogation reports and interrogation transcripts, POW rosters and transfer reports, interrogation log books, interrogation training materials, as well as graphic images and descriptions of Camp Tracy.

A second layer of information is interviews with former WWII U.S. service member veterans, who were stationed at Camp Tracy as interrogators, translators, and intelligence personnel, and the published memoirs of Japanese POWs, all of whom were interrogated at Camp Tracy. The personal interviews offer an oral history of Camp Tracy and strategic-level interrogation of Japanese POWs in WWII and provide a human perspective to complement the official documentation found at NARA. Since Camp Tracy was a top secret mission, the veterans, who are now in their 80s and 90s, did not take notes or write about their experiences in diaries, and in some cases had not spoken of their involvement at Camp Tracy until contacted by the author.

Chapter Two presents a review of literature about interrogation and the Japanese soldier's culture and mindset within a WWII context. This review also explores present-day interrogation to illustrate some of the difficulties that may be addressed through an examination of Camp Tracy. The objective is to provide a sense of the art and science of interrogation with an understanding of the Japanese concepts of honor and warrior ethos. Furthermore, this review demonstrates the difficulties that WWII interrogators faced, as well as draws parallels between WWII Japanese soldiers and current GWOT combatants.

Chapter Three describes the creation and operations of the Camp Tracy Joint Interrogation Center. It illustrates the process in which Camp Tracy came into existence, from the concept of a Joint Interrogation Center, to the site selection and construction of the facilities, and finally to the command structure of Camp Tracy itself. The objective here is to provide a basis of understanding for the reasoning behind a Joint Interrogation Center.

Chapter Four provides a detailed study of the interrogation process at Camp Tracy. It covers the entire interrogation process from the selection of the interrogators, to the selection of specific POWs for interrogation, to the conduct of the interrogation, to the means of gathering intelligence. The objective is to describe how WWII Camp Tracy interrogators accomplished their mission and the techniques they used to do so.

Chapter Five concludes this book with a composite list of lessons drawn from the Camp Tracy experience that can serve to inform interrogation policies, doctrine, and practices both today and in the future. This chapter also contains several recommendations for additional research on this subject.

Chapter 2

A Comparison

No good intelligence is going to come from abusive practices.
—Lieutenant General John F. Kimmons, U.S. Army[1]

While the current GWOT is being fought against an Islamist radical foe that seems alien and incomprehensible to most Americans, fortunately the United States has confronted in war and defeated such an enemy before. The foe was Japan and the war was, of course, WWII. One of the many parallels that can be drawn between today's jihadists and our Japanese adversaries of an earlier generation is the difficulty we faced then and currently face today in determining how best to exploit captured enemy combatants for the intelligence necessary to win the war. By looking back at how the United States handled interrogation operations against the Japanese, we can learn valuable lessons for organizing and executing interrogation operations in support of the GWOT.

A selective review of historical and contemporary literature is an essential first step in addressing the question: *What lessons can be learned from the experience of Camp Tracy, a U.S. strategic interrogation center for Japanese Prisoners of War during WWII, which can influence existing and future U.S. interrogation policies, doctrine, and practices?* The review rests on a representative sample of published first-hand accounts, academic studies, and historically relevant newspaper and magazine articles that focus on three areas that are essential to our investigation: current Joint Interrogation Centers (JICs); WWII interrogations of POWs in the European Theater; and the character of the WWII Japanese soldier.[2]

CURRENT "JOINT INTERROGATION CENTERS"

Before we can understand how the proposed question applies meaningfully to the GWOT, we must first examine some of the central issues surrounding JIC operations today. In that regard, the present-day JICs of Abu Ghraib, Iraq and Camp Delta, Cuba will be examined. The issues that arise out of those examinations are precisely the kinds of problems to which the successful resolution of our research can enable answers.

JIC at Abu Ghraib, Iraq

The recently published book *Monstering: Inside America's Policy of Secret Interrogations and Torture in the Terror War*, by Tara McKelvey, a senior editor at *The American Prospect*, offers a unique perspective on the operations at Forward Operating Base (FOB) Abu Ghraib, Iraq. McKelvey conducted interviews with the

Figure 2-1: Abu Ghraib Forward Operating Base, Iraq.

U.S. Army personnel who had instigated the events that resulted in the Abu Ghraib scandal; among those involved in the whole series of events were actual participants, such as Private First Class (PFC) Lindy England, and those who blew the whistle on the abuses, such as Sergeant (SGT) Samuel J. Provance III. In her book, McKelvey highlights two significant issues. The first is that U.S. Army personnel utilized during the events that occurred at Abu Ghraib were untrained. The participants were U.S. Army imagery intelligence (IMINT) analysts from Heidelberg, Germany, who had been given only a two-day crash course in interrogation operations.[3] It is unclear whether these IMINT analysts actually conducted any interrogations, but McKelvey indicates that they were eventually used as Military Intelligence Security or an "M.I. Guard Force," who assisted in the handling, transport, and security of the detainees. Allegations of mishandling and abuse arose from the actions of these analysts-turned-security force. According to McKelvey, SGT Provance stated that, "They'd [the MI Guard

Force] talk about their experience when the detainees were being humiliated and abused. It was like a joke story. It was like, 'Ha, ha. It was hilarious. You had to be there.'"[4]

The second serious issue that McKelvey raises is the U.S. decision to use Abu Ghraib prison as a JIC in the first place. She explains that the U.S. JIC was set up in the same facility where Saddam Hussein's regime had reportedly executed thousands of prisoners over the course of two decades from 1984 to 2001.[5] Under Hussein's regime, operations at the prison reportedly included rape rooms and torture chambers. While the prison was under U.S. control, on more than one occasion construction of new structures had to be halted during excavation operations because excavation crews had uncovered human skeletal remains.[6] According to McKelvey, the decision to make Abu Ghraib its main detention center and JIC now would be similar to a U.S. decision to use a Nazi concentration camp as a prison during WWII; McKelvey quotes a Coalition Provisional Authority (CPA) official as having stated, "It was no different than going into Dachau and saying, 'We're going to use this as a prison facility.'"[7]

Another key work that deals with the problems raised by the events that occurred at Abu Ghraib is *The Abu Ghraib Investigations: The Official Reports of the Independent Panel and the Pentagon on the Shocking Prisoner Abuse in Iraq*. Edited by Steven Strasser, this book consists of excerpts from the official investigations into Abu Ghraib's operations conducted by an independent panel, and by U.S. Army Major General (MG) George R. Fay. The independent panel, formed at the request of then-Secretary of Defense Donald H. Rumsfeld and chaired by former

Secretary of Defense James R. Schlesinger, emphasizes four noteworthy factors. The first was the massive overcrowding at the Abu Ghraib facility. By October 2003, Abu Ghraib housed up to seven thousand detainees with a guard force of only ninety U.S. Army military police.[8] This is a ratio of only one guard for every seventy-seven detainees.

The panel's second key issue relates to the physical location of the JIC and the combat-related consequences that arose from that location: "The choice of Abu Ghraib as the facility for detention operations placed a strictly detention mission-driven unit—one designed to operate in a rear area—smack in the middle of a combat environment."[9] During the month of July 2003, the JIC received mortar fire more than twenty-five times.[10] Between February 2004 and April 2004, the JIC was mortared every single day. The attacks subsided only after mortar fire on April 20, 2004, killed twenty-two detainees, wounded nearly one hundred more and turned Iraqi public opinion against the insurgent fighters.[11] These mortar attacks were facilitated by the fact that FOB Abu Ghraib is located between two major multi-lane roads to its north and south, which allows insurgents to launch several mortars and then speed away before Coalition forces could respond (see Figure 2-2).

The third relevant issue raised by the panel concerns the screening process at Abu Ghraib. Due to a lack of interrogators and interpreters on the front lines, during raid operations Coalition forces tended to round up everyone in the area targeted for the raid. These persons were then shipped to Abu Ghraib for the JIC's personnel to sort out. Because of the large numbers of people

© Google Earth.

Figure 2-2: FOB Abu Ghraib.

arriving at Abu Ghraib, detainees were in some cases held at the JIC for ninety days before being interrogated for the first time.[12] As time went by, the practice of delaying interrogations contributed significantly to prisoner-overcrowding at Abu Ghraib.

The fourth pertinent topic raised by the panel involves the use of civilian interrogators in JIC operations at the prison complex. Due to a shortage of U.S. military interrogators, contractors were hired to augment the military workforce. According to the panel, an inspection by the U.S. Army Inspector General found that thirty-five percent of the contracted "interrogators" had not received any formal training in U.S. military interrogation practices, policies, or doctrine.[13] Furthermore, the panel found evidence of poor military oversight of the contracted "interrogators" to ensure their methods were in compliance with established military regulations.

JIC at Camp Delta, Cuba

In contrast to the JIC at Abu Ghraib, Camp Delta is located on a U.S. military installation in Guantanamo, Cuba, which provides isolation and security for its detainees and military personnel (see Figure 2-3 below). An important account of events and operations occurring there has been provided by *Inside the Wire: A Military Intelligence Soldier's Eyewitness Account of Life at Guantanamo*, by Erik R. Saar and Viveca Novak. This book details the experience of SGT Erik Saar while he served as an interpreter at the Camp Delta JIC.

Figure 2-3: Camp Delta at Guantanamo, Cuba.

Saar, a former U.S. Army signals intelligence (SIGINT) analyst, provides three germane subjects to this review of appropriate literature. The first is the lack of proper detainee screening prior to their arrival at Camp Delta. Saar relates that as of

January 2003, there were nearly 100 detainees identified who should never have been sent to Camp Delta in the first place.[14] Explaining how some of the "innocent" detainees arrived at the JIC, Saar provides an explanation given by one of the detainees: "'the Northern Alliance moved in and took away every Arab man in the area...they [the Northern Alliance] took us to their own prison for a few days...finally, we were turned over to the Americans.'"[15]

Saar's second topic-of-concern is the lack of cultural awareness of the interrogators at Camp Delta. He explains that before someone can understand the detainees and make headway in questioning or interrogating them, that person must have a firm grasp of the detainees' cultural and religious beliefs. Based on his experiences at Camp Delta, Saar asserts that, "What too many interrogators didn't seem to understand was the sustaining power of the detainees' commitment to their faith."[16]

Saar's third issue is the increasing number of contract-interrogators at Camp Delta. As with Abu Ghraib, the contractors at Camp Delta lacked the same level of experience or training as their military counterparts. Saar relates, "There didn't seem to be a terribly rigorous vetting process for these hires, judging by what we saw."[17] He provides an example of a female contract-interrogator who, believing that the detainees were drawing strength from their religious beliefs, attempted to make a detainee feel impure by disrobing and conducting the interrogation wearing just a bra and a thong.[18]

WWII INTERROGATIONS OF EUROPEAN POWS

To move forward in our search for a solution, we need to consider how interrogations have been successfully conducted in the past. *The British Empire and its Italian Prisoners of War, 1940-1947*, by Bob Moore and Kent Fedorowich, catalogs the British experience with Italian POWs during WWII in the European, African, and Pacific Theaters. While Moore and Fedorowich relate meaningful details concerning interrogations of Italian POWs, they focus their efforts on the ways in which the Italian POWs were "co-opted" into the British war effort, primarily by filling shortages in the British agricultural labor force. Moore and Fedorowich write, "These [Italian] prisoners were prized by various government departments as a docile but potentially invaluable source of labour."[19] Such a use of POWs was made possible by the shared European culture and value-sets of the Italians and the British.

Conversely, in the United States, WWII Japanese POWs were kept secured in POW camps throughout the entire war. An article that appeared in the April 1944 edition of the *Science Digest* details an American sentiment of the time: "The Jap prisoner can seldom be trusted to work or do the other things his partners, the Germans, do willingly."[20] The only exception to this policy of Japanese prisoner-containment occurred when, for a short period of two months before their eventual repatriation from the continental United States, Japanese POWs worked in cotton fields at a POW Camp in Lamont, California.[21] It is similarly difficult to imagine the United States being willing to utilize currently held GWOT adversaries in domestic labor pools.

Although another set of recently declassified WWII documents, that details the operation of a German POW camp in England, provides interesting information, that information is largely irrelevant for purposes of this study. As described in *Camp 020: MI5 and the Nazi Spies*, edited by Oliver Hoare, Camp 020 was located in the London Borough of Richmond during WWII, and had the mission of interrogating and "turning" suspected German agents who had been captured in England.[22] While an excellent source of study concerning WWII interrogation techniques and counterintelligence operations, Camp 020 primarily dealt with English-speaking German prisoners who had been caught attempting to assimilate into English society.[23] However, physical, cultural, linguistic, and religious differences between the German prisoners and their English captors were practically non-existent; therefore, a study of Camp 020 does not lend itself to a meaningful comparison between the United States and its adversaries in the GWOT today.

THE WWII JAPANESE SOLDIER AND GWOT ISLAMISTS

WWII research on German and Italian POWs can provide a good understanding of the basics of interrogation practices utilized at that time. However, because of the physical, cultural, linguistic, and religious similarities between the Allied powers and the European Axis partners, there is not much valuable information to assist in successful prosecution of the GWOT today. To fully grasp the possible WWII lessons that can aid in today's fight in the GWOT, we must look beyond the European Axis powers of Italy and Germany, and instead focus on their Far Eastern Axis partner, Japan.

Japanese "Emperor Worship"

As this study has already indicated, there were vast differences between the U.S. and Japanese cultures. U.S. Air Force (USAF) Captain James A. Stone discusses some of these in his National Defense Intelligence College thesis entitled "Interrogation of Japanese POWs in WWII: U.S. Response to a Formidable Challenge." In this work, Captain Stone explains that a key aspect of WWII-era Japanese psychology was its focus on the Imperial Family, which was manifested by Emperor Worship. Stone relates that the Japanese "attributed their extreme militarism to the Emperor and claimed they were 'carrying out his will' and 'dying at the Emperor's command.'"[24]

This almost inexplicable devotion of the Japanese to their Emperor finds support in John W. Dower's book *War Without Mercy: Race & Power in the Pacific War*. Dower asserts that the Japanese soldiers fought with incredibly fierce tenacity, frequently conducting open frontal assaults on American positions in a berserk rampage, screaming *Tennōheika Banzai*! ("Long Live the Emperor!") as they were ripped apart by American gunfire.[25] One explanation of Japanese fanaticism comes from the 1942 *Reader's Digest* article, "Close Up of the Jap Fighting Man," in which U.S. Army Lieutenant Colonel (LTC) Warren J. Clear, an infantry officer who spent four years learning Japanese and training with the Japanese Army prior to WWII, explains that based on his observations the Japanese view the Emperor as "the Son of Heaven, the Supreme Being, an incarnate god."[26]   LTC Clear further accounts of instances in which Japanese would rush into burning buildings to save the Emperor's portrait; that school principals confronted with a choice between letting children perish in a school fire and attempting to retrieve the Emperor's portrait not only chose the portrait over the children, but also committed *seppuku*, also known as *hara-kiri*, ("ritual suicide") if they survived the fire but failed to retrieve the portrait.[27]

Japanese worship of their Emperor as a deity incarnate is evident in other dramatic, but less-tragic forms of social behavior. In *War Against Japan*, Sidney C. Moody Jr. writes that devotion to the Emperor is so engrained in the Japanese people that they would turn their backs to the Emperor as he passed to avoid touching his transcendent royal person with their commoner eyes.[28]   According to Ruth Benedict in *The Chrysanthemum and the Sword: Patterns of Japanese Culture*, all windows above the first floor were closed and shuttered as the Emperor passed by to ensure that no one could look down upon the Emperor.[29]   In his analysis of "Emperor Worship," Moody indicates that this notion was encouraged by the military-dominated Japanese cabinet, which effectively ran the Japanese government, in its efforts to build and define the national identity and spirit.   This worshipful attitude led to the *banzai* ("10,000 years") combat charges during which Japanese soldiers offered 10,000 years of glory to the Emperor as they attacked their enemies in human wave after human wave in the Emperor's name.[30]

Islamic Dedication to the Glory of Allah

This same sense of blind devotion, reverence, and fanaticism that the Japanese exhibited during WWII can also be seen in the actions of Islamist radicals that the United States is battling today. These radicals may manifest their zeal by following a particular charismatic figure such as Osama bin Laden, or radical Muslim clerics such as Omar Abdel Rahmen, the so-called "Blind Sheikh," who was convicted in the first World Trade Center bombing conspiracy. Or, more generally, such Islamist radicals might devote their energies to "carrying out God's will," as defined by these or other charismatic figures. Either path the fanatic chooses, the results are the same. The enemy combatants of GWOT shout with fervor *Allahu Akbar* ("Allah is Great") as they carry out their attacks against their enemies—Western infidels or apostate Muslims.

For example, Mohammed Atta, the hijacker who flew American Airlines Flight 11 into the north tower of the World Trade Center on September 11, 2001, (9/11) had left behind a document detailing the steps for the attack. In the third, or execution, phase of the 9/11 attack, he instructs his fellow Islamists, "hit like heroes who do not want to return back to life. Shout '*Allahu Akbar.*'"[31] Likewise, when the hijackers of United Airlines Flight 93 were thwarted in reaching their original targets of the U.S. Capitol Building or the White House by passengers on the plane who rose up against them, they decided to crash their plane into a Pennsylvania field. As the plane plummeted toward the ground, the hijackers shouted, "*Allahu Akbar! Allahu Akbar!*"[32]

Japanese Suicidal Missions

If fear, awe, and love of their Emperor were feelings inculcated in the Japanese from infancy on, those feelings certainly found their most dramatic expression in the suicide missions undertaken by

Japanese pilots during WWII. There were, however, additional reasons for these missions. Edwin M. Nakasone devotes an entire chapter to the subject of Japanese WWII *Kamikaze* ("Divine Wind") pilot tactics in his book *The Nisei Soldier: Historical Essays on World War II and the Korean War.*[33] Nakasone explains that six factors influenced Japanese youth to volunteer to become *Kamikaze* pilots. The first was the *Bushido* ("samurai") Code that had been revived as part of the Meiji Restoration in the nineteenth century and had subsequently been taught to all Japanese from birth. This code comprises principles of "honor, courage, loyalty, the ability to endure pain, self sacrifice, reverence for the Emperor and contempt of death."[34] Nakasone explains that the principles of the *Bushido* Code were altered somewhat by the Japanese government and were then made a central part of the Japanese national ideology. According to this ideology, dying for the Emperor was the single most glorious and important action in which a Japanese citizen could engage.[35]

The second causative factor Nakasone introduces is the concept of religious principles. He contends that most Japanese youth held strong religious convictions whose central tenet was the concept that self-sacrifice led to spiritual elevation, allowing them to join the ranks of their venerated ancestors. By capitalizing on these religious convictions, the Japanese government advanced the *Kamikaze* pilot as a role model and hero for all Japanese people.[36]

The third factor that contributed to the Japanese embrace of suicide missions, according to Nakasone, was the culture's martial traditions. He asserts that Japanese youth were trained from an early age in the warrior ethos and martial traditions. Therefore, becoming a *Kamikaze* pilot was the highest calling and ultimate expression of the warrior tradition: to die defending the Emperor.[37]

The fourth factor that Nakasone's identifies was the cold logic of force-ratios. He argues that some Japanese youth volunteered to become *Kamikaze* pilots with the understanding that one Japanese pilot could destroy an entire American ship by crashing into it. Exchanging a single plane for a ship was therefore mathematically and logically the right thing to do.[38]

The fifth factor that persuaded young Japanese men to embrace suicide missions was the tradition of avoiding *haji* ("shame"). Nakasone asserts that a common cultural belief was that it was better for Japanese youth to die than accept shame, so suicide was considered an honorable act. By bravely dying in the Emperor's name, the Japanese *Kamikaze* pilots avoided bringing shame to themselves or their family, and instead brought great honor.[39]

The final factor that influenced young Japanese men to volunteer to become *Kamikaze* pilots in WWII, according to Nakasone, was the national philosophy of obedience and rejection of individualism. To the Japanese, the individual was less important than the group. While rejecting and rooting out thoughts of individualism, the Japanese government at the same time perpetuated a philosophy of obedience and reverence to the Emperor. Inculcating such concepts allowed the Japanese leadership to reinforce the attitude that dying for country and Emperor was the right thing to do.[40]

Additional insights into the Japanese suicide missions are provided by Dower in his book, *War Without Mercy*. Dower explains that the suicidal attacks were based on the concept of *gyokusai* ("jewel smashed") from a sixth-century Japanese story whose lesson is that a great man should die as a shattered jewel rather than live as an intact tile. He also notes that *Kamikaze* pilots traditionally wore white Rising Sun headbands, white scarves, and white *senninbari* ("thousand-stitch belts") in which a thousand women had each sewn one stitch to symbolically join the men in their final sacrifice.[41] Donning clean clothes and drinking a ritual cup of water as an act of purification, the *Kamikazes* embarked on their mission to serve as "fire-arrow deities" sacrificing their lives to cleanse a polluted world.[42]

Islamist Suicide Bombers

Islamist suicide bombers share several commonalities with WWII Japanese *Kamikaze* pilots as Nasra Hassan explains in *An Arsenal of Believers: Talking to the "Human Bombs."* The Islamic concept of *shaheed* ("martyr" or "witness") holds that Muslims who sacrifice themselves to strike at the enemy are assured a place in God's Paradise. Would-be martyrs usually spend months, sometimes years, in religious studies, which could be construed as a form of indoctrination, before they are selected to become a martyr. Once selected, the *al shaheed al hayy* ("the living martyr") undergoes further religious studies and spiritual exercises in preparation for the attack. Before setting out on the holy mission, the *al shaheed al hayy* performs a ritual act of purification, shaves excess body hair, attires his body in clean clothes, and attempts to attend one last prayer service at a mosque.[43]

While this concept of *shaeed* is not part of the religious beliefs of every young male Muslim, it is pervasive enough to wonder what factors attract such followers. To give an answer to this question, as part of her research conducted from 1996 to 1999, Hassan interviewed nearly 250 Islamists involved in suicidal bombing attacks. During one interview, she asked an Islamist who survived his own "sacred explosion," what the attraction was in martyrdom.[44] He responded, "Someone bent on martyrdom becomes immune to the material pull...we were floating, swimming, in the feeling that we were about to enter eternity. We had no doubts. We made an oath on the Koran, in the presence of Allah—a pledge not to waver...I know that there are other ways to do jihad. But this one is sweet—the sweetest."[45] When asked how he felt when he was selected for martyrdom, he replied, "It's as if a very high, impenetrable wall separated you from Paradise or Hell. Allah has promised one or the other to his creatures. So, by pressing the detonator, you can immediately open the door to Paradise—it is the shortest path to Heaven."[46]

Reliance on Spirit and Faith

As Benedict explains in *The Chrysanthemum and the Sword*, the Japanese government portrayed the war against America as a conflict between faiths. Japan had faith in the spirit while the United States had faith in matter, or physical objects. Therefore, it did not matter that the United States had more military materiel, because Americans did not have the Japanese spirit which would ultimately prevail. Benedict summarizes this feeling in the statement that Japanese "soldiers were taught that death itself was a victory of the spirit."[47] Meirion and Susie Harries, authors of *Soldiers of the Sun: The Rise and Fall of the Imperial Japanese*

Army, would agree with this assessment. The Harries write that, as the war dragged on, spirit was heavily relied on to compensate for the decreasing levels of training, poor quality of equipment, and suspect caliber of conscripted soldiers that made up the Imperial Army. They note that there were four tons of equipment available for every American soldier in the field during the war in the Pacific Theater, compared with only two pounds for every Japanese soldier.[48]

The Harries also indicate that this reliance on spirit and faith included the Japanese soldiers' willingness to die, a phenomenon they refer to as "a legacy of the authentic samurai ethic, as the war progressed acceptance of death became ever more heavily stressed—just as it was ever more necessary."[49] The Japanese did not have the resources to combat the Americans and therefore had to resort to the use of suicide tactics. One example was the use of Japanese soldiers with a live-fused 550 pound (250 kilograms) bomb between their knees and a brick in their hand waiting for a tank to roll by and thereby serving as human improvised explosive devices (IEDs).[50]

Today's Islamists find themselves in a situation similar to that of WWII Japanese soldiers. Ami Pedahzur explains in *Suicide Terrorism* that Al Qaeda was forced to use asymmetric suicide tactics against the United States, a world superpower, because of its limited resources. Pedahzur further explains how prospective martyrs are recruited by emphasizing the *shaheed*'s ability to serve as an advocate for his family members in heaven on Judgment Day.[51]

Demonization of the Enemy

In response to the surprise bombing of Pearl Harbor, the American public began demonizing the Japanese people as a whole, while discriminating between Germans and Nazis, as Dower explains in *War Without Mercy*. According to Dower, it was possible to have "good Germans" who were not Nazis, but no such discriminations were made about the Japanese: all Japanese were "bad." The WWII Commander of U.S. South Pacific Force, Admiral William F. Halsey, encapsulated that attitude in a statement he made in a press conference early on in the war: "The only good Jap is a Jap who's been dead six months."[52] Demonization of the Japanese people included characterizing them as less than human; in such characterizations, they appeared as inferior creatures like monkeys or as an infestation of lice (see Figures 2-4 and 2-5).

By David Low, © Solo Syndication.

Figure 2-4: Difference Between Japanese Monkey-man and Western Allies.

Louseous Japanicas

The first serious outbreak of this lice epidemic was officially noted on December 7, 1941, at Honolulu, T. H. To the Marine Corps, especially trained in combating this type of pestilence, was assigned the gigantic task of extermination. Extensive experiments on Guadalcanal, Tarawa, and Saipan have shown that this louse inhabits coral atolls in the South Pacific, particularly pill boxes, palm trees, caves, swamps and jungles.

Flame throwers, mortars, grenades and bayonets have proven to be an effective remedy. But before a complete cure may be effected the origin of the plague, the breeding grounds around the Tokyo area, must be completely annihilated.

"Bugs Every Marine Should Know," © Leatherneck.

Figure 2-5: Depiction of Japanese as Lice.

Dower explains that the Japanese in turn portrayed the Americans as barbaric animals, intent on destroying "the divine state of Japan" merely to sate their carnal urges.[53] Americans, who were depicted as sub-human, commonly "killed deformed babies by drowning them, and…even practiced infanticide by smashing their baby's head against a wall."[54] Anti-American, government-sponsored propaganda told the Japanese people that American children were being brainwashed to kill Japanese, and this propaganda helped spread a "kill-or-be-killed" mentality within Japan. Additional propaganda included stories about Americans driving tanks over wounded Japanese soldiers, wrapping sick Japanese in concertina wire and tossing them into rivers. Most alarming to the Japanese public, however, was their government's claim that Americans "took pleasure in playing with the sacred bones of the Japanese war dead."[55] Borrowing from the country's folklore, Japanese propaganda utilized such icons as the divinely born *Momotarō* to fight the enemy (see Figure 2-6), while also commonly representing Allied leadership as demons or devils (see Figure 2-7).

By Yukio Sugiura, © Jun Sugiura.

Figure 2-6: Japanese Folklore Icon *Momotarō*, Slaying Churchill and Roosevelt (Depicted as Demons).

Figure 2-7: Roosevelt the Demon Showing His True Face.

It should not come as a surprise, then, that fighting in the Pacific was more brutal than fighting in the European Theater.

Such rhetoric drove emotions high on both sides of the conflict. Even after fighting the Japanese for nearly four years, U.S. servicemen still believed that "the only good Jap is a dead one." This attitude made the capture of Japanese POWs for interrogation nearly impossible. SGT Ozzie St. George in *Yank: The Army Weekly* explains that during its campaign on Luzon in the Philippines, the 32d U.S. Army Division recognized this problem and resorted to a new ploy: its new policy was that, "any GI who brought in a Jap, reasonably alive and capable of talking, was rewarded with a case of beer and a three-day pass."[56]

Let's turn our attention now to similar feelings and similar denunciations in our own time. Following the 9/11 attacks, there were verbal attacks against Islamists but not against Muslims as a whole. This distinction is due in part to the actions of U.S. leaders who diligently worked to delineate the differences for the American people between the Islamic religion and the Islamists who carried out the 9/11 attacks. For example, President Bush made a public appearance on September 17, 2001, at the Islamic Center of Washington in an attempt to prevent any hate crimes or discrimination against Muslims and Arab-Americans. The President explained that the 9/11 attacks violated the tenets and fundamentals of Islam: "the face of terror is not the true faith of Islam. That's not what Islam is all about. Islam is peace. These terrorists don't represent peace. They represent evil and war."[57]

In spite of the efforts of governmental leaders, however, it is still hard for some Americans to make a distinction between Muslims and Islamists due to the emotional scars from 9/11. Nor is the fear and distrust confined to the American side. Saar, the author of *Inside the Wire*, who is a trained Arabic linguist, described his feelings when he confronted detainees—most of whom were eventually proven to be guiltless and released—at Camp Delta: "I was about to walk into the midst of nearly fifty men, all bound by an alleged hate for the United States, who I had no doubt would kill me if they had the chance. Some of them may have helped plan the hijacking of those planes."[58]

Language Barriers

Another area of similarity between WWII Japanese soldiers and Islamist radicals is the seemingly impenetrable nature of the language. According to Joseph D. Harrington in *Yankee Samurai: The Secret Role of Nisei in America's Pacific Victory*, Japanese is perhaps the hardest language in the world for foreigners to learn. The reason is that Japanese, which was adopted in the sixth century, is a "picture word" system based originally on the Chinese language. Each "picture," or ideograph, which is called a *kanji*, received a new meaning in Japanese. Throughout the centuries since, additional nuances, subtleties, and variations were incorporated to the point that each *kanji* now has as many as twenty-five different interpretations. Further complications arose through linguistic modifications that reflected the status of the person speaking with regard to the status of the listener, as well as the subject of their discussion. Harrington asserts that "even someone who knows the language very well cannot always be sure either of what he is saying, or that he is being understood."[59]

An additional difficulty that communicating in Japanese presents comes from the abbreviated styles of writing Japanese script called *gyosho* and *soshu*. In *Interrogation of Japanese POWs in WWII*, author Stone characterizes the similarity between these two cursive writing styles and the printed Japanese character as the similarity between a shorthand symbol and a printed word in English.[60]

The written form of the Arabic language can be just as perplexing to a native English speaker now as Japanese was during WWII. Arabic consists of 28 letters that are written in four distinct forms depending on the position of the letter in the word—whether at its beginning, middle, end or non-connected (also known as isolated or independent). To complicate matters, Arabic has different ways to abbreviate or "shorthand" a letter that make the letter written by hand look completely different from the same letter when it has been printed. Finally, Arabic typically uses a cursive Semitic script, but many other artistic forms of the script abound. All are written from right to left, the opposite of English and other Western languages.

Aside from the script, written Arabic is especially challenging for Westerners because of its tri-consonantal, root-based system from which words are formed. Its difficulty is compounded by having ten different verb "measures" where some verbs appear to have the same spelling, but have different meanings based on the pronunciation. The chart that follows, illustrates the complexity of the conjugation of the ten measures (see Figure 2-8 below). Additionally, the language is only minimally literal; it is filled with figurative allusions, which are probably based upon its rich oral traditions. For example, in Arabic there is only one word for snow but over two hundred for sand.[61]

© *Bahgat W. Malek.*

Figure 2-8: The Ten Measures of the Triliteral Arab Verb.

Spoken Arabic commonly is dialectical from country to country throughout the Middle East and North Africa, and also includes distinct subdialects within individual countries. These dialects often include different words for the same meaning as well as different styles of pronunciations. Such differences have meaningful linguistic and communication consequences. For example, an Arab from Lebanon and an Arab from Morocco are more likely to use either French or English to communicate instead of trying to get past their Arabic dialectical differences.[62]

Japanese Warrior Ethos/Military Culture

A final similarity between WWII Japanese soldiers and the GWOT adversaries of today is the presence and significance of a military culture or warrior ethos in the lives of both. According to Hanson W. Baldwin, a 1943 Pulitzer Prize recipient for his Southwest Pacific WWII coverage, in *This is the Army We Have to Defeat; a Picture of the Japanese Soldier and the Organization of Which He is the Core*, the Japanese male underwent extreme military training and indoctrination before becoming a soldier. He would fight to the death for two reasons: the fear of bringing disgrace and shame upon his family; and a blind obedience to customs, traditions, duties, and orders instilled in him. Baldwin explains that "Japanese fighting men are subjected to an intense chauvinistic orientation and 'spiritual training' with emphasis upon physical hardihood and endurance and loyalty unto death."[63] He predicted that the Japanese Army would cost America heavily in blood and tears before the war ended, in part because "the average Japanese soldier is tough, for he is raised and trained from childhood to be tough, to endure pain without whimpering, to get used to hardship, to put Emperor and nation far ahead of life."[64]

Other researchers/writers would agree with Baldwin's assessment of the mindset of the Japanese soldier. In *Close Up*, Clear relates that "the modern Jap soldier is the product of centuries of internecine warfare that made the island kingdom one vast blood-soaked battlefield."[65] He, like other authors referred to in this study, explains that the warrior ethos was ingrained into the Japanese from their childhood. By age twelve, Japanese males were in uniform participating in military exercises. By age fifteen, they trained with the bayonet. At age sixteen, they practiced driving mock tanks. By nineteen, they marched twenty-five miles a day with a full combat pack.[66] In a way of quantifying the mettle of the Japanese, Clear describes an example of an exercise executed by the Japanese regiment that he trained with: in pouring rain, carrying full combat loads, the men marched 122 miles in 72 hours with only four hours of sleep, and ended the march at the double-time.[67] When he spoke with the regimental commander about the decision to finish the march at the double-time, the commander replied, "Tired men can always march one more mile to take another enemy position."[68] Clear summarizes the grueling three-day march as one that, "no other army in the world could have endured."[69]

Another author further illustrates the nature of extreme discipline and warrior-like mentality induced in soldiers in the Japanese Army. Benedict in *The Chrysanthemum and the Sword* describes orders given by an officer to his soldiers during military-training maneuvers not to drink from their canteens before they set out on a forced fifty-mile road march. Twenty men collapsed during the march from heat exhaustion and dehydration, and five men eventually died. Later, an inspection of their canteens revealed that despite their dehydration, all of the canteens were full and untouched.[70]

Islamist Warrior Heritage

The Bedouin inhabitants of the Arabian Peninsula, who would become the first Muslims, had a long warrior tradition prior to the emergence of Islam. Although the Bedouin tribes practiced agriculture, herding, and trading, they also routinely engaged in intertribal warfare as a primary means of obtaining livestock and goods.[71] As William L. Cleveland explains in *A History of the Middle East*, "All [Bedouin] males were expected to be warriors, and accounts of the exploits of the most daring among them became enshrined in tribal culture."[72] However, the introduction of Islam and the *Quran* in the seventh century unified the Arabian Peninsula, and halted the practice of intertribal warfare. John L. Esposito explains, in his book *Islam: The Straight Path*, that Muslims "were bound by a common faith and committed to the creation of a socially just society."[73]

As part of the Islamic faith, Muslims are obligated to propagate and spread Islam to the rest of the non-Islamic world. Majid Khadduri explains in *War and Peace in the Law of Islam*, that "it is the duty of...every believer not only to see that God's word shall be supreme, but also that no infidel shall deny God or be ungrateful for His favors."[74] Islam transformed the newly converted Bedouins into zealous Islamic warriors who, compelled to spread the word of God, eventually conquered their way across the Middle East, North Africa, and parts of Europe and Indonesia. Esposito explains:

> They spread a way of life...acknowledging the ultimate sovereignty of God, living according to His law, obeying His Prophet, and dedicating their lives to spreading God's rule and law. This was the message and vision that accompanied Arab Armies as they burst out of Arabia and established their supremacy.[75]

By the mid-eighth century, only a little over one hundred years after Prophet Muhammad's death, the Islamic Empire had spread to three continents (see Figure 2-9). Not only was the Islamic Empire expanding rapidly but it was flourishing while Europe was mired in the "Dark Ages." As J.J. Saunders explains in *A History of Medieval Islam*, "For more than four hundred years the most fruitful work in mathematics, astronomy, botany, chemistry, medicine, history and geography, was produced in the world of Islam by Muslims."[76]

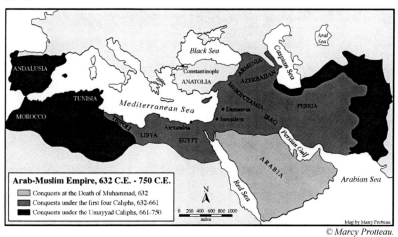

© *Marcy Protteau.*

Figure 2-9: The Arab-Muslim Empire 632 C.E. – 750 C.E.

Today, Islamists are painfully aware of how far they have fallen behind Europe and the West and yearn for a return to their great past, the "Golden Age" of Islamic supremacy.[77] As Fawaz A. Gerges explains in *Journey of the Jihadist: Inside Muslim Militancy*, the goal of the Islamists "is to dismantle the secular authoritarian order that succeeded British and French colonialism after World War II," and reestablish the Islamic Empire.[78] To Islamist leaders such as Osama bin Laden, this yearning provides an entry point for anti-Western, pro-Islamist ideology to tap into the Muslim consciousness and to fan the embers of the great Islamic warrior heritage back into a roaring flame.[79]

As with the Japanese, this awakening is accomplished through the initiation of military and religious indoctrination during childhood. Joyce M. Davis explains in *Martyrs: Innocence, Vengeance, and Despair in the Middle East*, that in some cases

Muslim children, from ages five to fifteen, undergo weapons training to learn how to "shoot Kalashnikovs and explode hand grenades."[80]   Muslim children are routinely exposed to Islamist teachings in their mosques and *maddrassas* ("religious-based schools").[81]   By practicing rote memorization of the *Quran* with literal and Islamist interpretations, young Muslims absorb teachings that Islamists can use to instill in them hatred of the West and a longing for Islamic ascension.[82]

Davis continues onto explain that those students who seem truly "devout" and show promise for further indoctrination are recruited by the Islamists.[83]   These recruits are sent to military-styled training camps where two significant things happen: (1) their dedication and devotion to the Islamist cause is more deeply inculcated, and (2) they are provided with the military skills necessary to channel that dedication against the "enemies of Islam."[84]   These intensive religious and militaristic experiences in the training camps convert the Muslims to active Islamists, ready to fight and die for the Islamist cause as directed.[85]

This literature review has suggested several key similarities between the WWII Japanese soldiers and the Islamist radicals of today. The most significant of these are the following: a fanatical or fervent sense of worship, willingness to participate in suicide operations, negative U.S. perceptions, an alien-like language, and a warrior-like culture or heritage.   Consequently, through a determination of the ways in which Camp Tracy interrogators were able to educe information from the Japanese POWs, valuable information can be gleaned to provide instructive lessons in the United States' struggle in the current GWOT.

Chapter 3

Camp Tracy, P.O. Box 651

The main building is constructed by brick. There is nothing distinctive or attractive about its appearance. It is merely a four-story box-like structure with various wings.
—Captain Earl L. Edwards' description of the Byron Hot Springs Resort[1]

The initial push for a U.S. strategic-level interrogation center during WWII was from the U.S. Navy. The Office of Naval Intelligence (ONI) had studied a British interrogation facility located near London for a period of six months in 1941 and liked what it saw.[2] ONI found that a strategic-level interrogation center offered many advantages over individual interrogations of POWs at the time and place of their capture. One major advantage was that a central interrogation facility provided a "greater certainty for obtaining proper results from the interrogation of captured submarine crews, airman, and...army prisoners."[3] Based on the Navy's recommendation, and with the Army's concurrence, the Secretary of War approved the creation of two joint U.S. Army and Navy interrogation centers.[4]

Joint Interrogation Centers (JIC) were formed partly because of a previous agreement between the Army and Navy which stipulated that POWs would remain in naval custody for only as long as it took to transfer them to Army custody.[5] By setting up the facility as a JIC under the command and control of the Army, the Navy met the conditions of the prior agreement and at the same time retained access to the POWs that were of interest to the Navy. A second benefit of a *Joint* Interrogation Center was burden-sharing; both services supplied personnel required to man and run the JIC instead of only one. This allowed the Army and Navy to deploy the limited number of available qualified interrogators forward into the European and Pacific Theaters for the tactical mission, without sacrificing any capabilities at the strategic level.[6]

SITE SELECTION

The first JIC was established on the East Coast at Fort Hunt, Virginia; its primary purpose was the interrogation of European POWs.[7] The second JIC was to be established on the West Coast, preferably in the vicinity of San Francisco or Los Angles, primarily to interrogate Japanese POWs.[8] The task of determining a suitable site for the West Coast JIC fell to Army Infantry Captain (CPT) Earl L. Edwards.

On April 15, 1942, CPT Edwards traveled to the Presidio of San Francisco, California; for three days CPT Edwards inspected potential sites and met with local realtors to identify suitable locations. He used the following criteria to make his selections: proximity to San Francisco, adequacy of existing facilities, privacy, availability, and space for further construction. After concluding his inspection tour, CPT Edwards recommended four locations, all in California, in this order: (1) Byron Hot Springs, (2) The Olympic Club at Lakeside, (3) Ko-Noc-Ti, and (4) Carolands.[9] According to CPT Edwards' report on the first choice, Byron Hot Springs:

1. Col. John Weckerling, Assistant Chief of Staff, G-2, recommends the use of "Byron Hot Springs" as an interrogation center because of the luxury and popularity of various baths among the Japanese. He believes these would be most conducive to "softening up" Japanese prisoners of war.
2. The property is sufficiently near to San Francisco.
3. Sufficient existing construction is present and adaptable to use as an interrogation center.
4. Isolation and guarding features are outstanding.
5. The property can be adapted to profound uses with a minimum expenditure of time.
6. There may be little or no cost in acquiring the property.
7. It is doubtful that the buildings or the land would [*sic*] any salvage value after the war.
8. "Byron Hot Springs" is the best suited of all the properties inspected.

Recommendation.

That "Byron Hot Springs" be acquired for use as an interrogation center immediately.[10]

The U.S. Army Provost Marshal General approved CPT Edwards' recommendation on May 1, 1942, and the Army took possession of the property on June 1, 1942.[11]

SITE CONSTRUCTION

Named for its natural hot salt springs, Byron Hot Springs Resort was founded in 1865 but actually predates the nearby town of Byron by thirteen years.[12] Located only 54 miles east of San Francisco, the resort has long served as a health spa and retreat. The first hotel, built on the site in 1878, was destroyed in a fire on July 25, 1901.[13] The second hotel, built on the site in 1902, was also destroyed in a fire on July 18, 1912.[14] The third hotel, a four-story fireproof brick and concrete building built in 1914, was the building CPT Edwards inspected in 1942 (see Figure 3-1 below).[15]

© Kim Romena.

Figure 3-1: Byron Hot Springs Resort Hotel, Site of the Camp Tracy JIC.[16]

During the next six months, the Army modified the hotel for use as a JIC, including the installation of almost $50,000 worth of various "technical apparatus," which included twenty state-of-the-art Memovox transcriber recorders, five Memovox recorder and reproducer instruments (see Figure 3-2 below), 100 microphones, and miles of wire.[17]

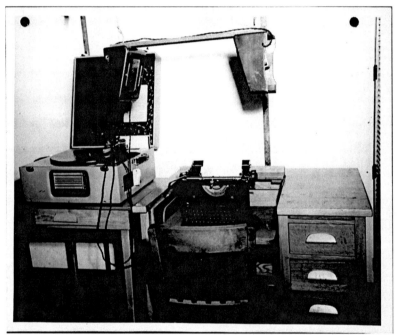

National Archives and Records Administration.
Figure 3-2: Memovox Recorder and Reproducing Machine.

These devices were used to record, copy, and transcribe POW interrogations and conversations for intelligence purposes.[18]

Another $50,000 was spent on the construction of new buildings and on retrofitting the hotel for interrogation operations. As part of that retrofitting, the entire top floor (22 rooms) was specially prepared to serve as POW living quarters. This generous amount of prisoner housing allowed 44 POWs to be held at the JIC at one time.[19] Securing the POWs was of paramount importance.

Courtesy of the Tracy Historical Society.
Figure 3-3: Outside View of Camp Tracy Interrogation Center.

The windows in the POW rooms were replaced with heavy wire mesh glass with metal bars (see Figure 3-3 above), and the doors were replaced with heavy prison-style doors, each featuring a small sliding slot, bars and special locks. The overhead dome-light, the only source of electrical light in each room, was rewired so that the sole light switch was in the hallway.[20]

While these modifications seem straightforward and logical, when we consider the rooms would house prisoners, the next two modifications were extremely unusual and quite clever. As a ruse, false ceilings were installed in the POW rooms and adjoining bathrooms, and ventilation grates were placed in the bathrooms. These bathroom vents allowed POWs to easily communicate with POWs in the next room. Normally, as per current POW handling doctrine found in U.S. Army Field Manual 2-22.3 (*Human Intelligence Collector Operations*), prisoners are to be kept silent so they cannot plan any deception or encourage one another to resist. In this case, however, interrogators preferred that prisoners speak to each other because microphones installed in the false ceilings (see Figure 3-4 below) allowed the interrogators to listen in on the prisoners' "private" conversations.[21]

Courtesy of Sam Matthews, Tracy Press.

Figure 3-4: In a 1969 Visit, Frank Shelby, U.S. Navy Chief Petty Officer Formerly Stationed at Camp Tracy, Points to the False Ceilings.

The third floor of the hotel was divided up between four interrogation rooms and ten rooms for the interrogators' living quarters. As in the prisoners' living areas, the interrogation rooms also had false ceilings which were wired with microphones.[22] The wiring of the interrogation rooms for sound allowed intelligence personnel in other parts of the building to monitor the interrogations, as well as to produce complete transcripts and recordings.[23]

The second floor of the JIC housed the remaining interrogation officers and provided kitchen and dining areas for the U.S. personnel. While there were little or no changes to this floor's existing structure, other aspects of the first floor were extensively modified. Four rooms on the first floor were sound-proofed with acoustic tiles to serve as special "play back" rooms that allowed interrogators to listen to POW interrogation and room monitoring recordings.[24] An additional two rooms, known as the "M" Rooms, served as the recording and monitoring nucleus for all of the microphones in the interrogation rooms and POW living quarters.[25] The monitoring equipment was manned from 0700 to 2200 hours every day unless there were "special circumstances" that necessitated additional monitoring.[26] The interrogators' administrative offices were also located on this floor.[27]

Interestingly, the receiving and processing room for POWs was also on the first floor. The location of the POW in-processing station provides another explanation as to why the "play back" rooms were sound-proofed—the interrogators did not want POWs who were bring in-processed to learn about the electronic monitoring. To expedite POW in-processing, a hole had been cut in the outer rear wall of the building and a door installed.[28] The receiving room was located next to the service stairs so that POWs could be quickly and efficiently moved to their new rooms after their in-processing and subsequently secured. Heavy metal doors with special locks had replaced the former doors leading off from the service stairs. These doors helped to facilitate and control the flow of POWs from the receiving room to their living quarters, and to and from their interrogations on the third floor.[29]

The resort itself also underwent some changes relative to its wartime use. As seen in Figure 3-5 (building #2), a fence with four guard posts (#31-34) at each corner was constructed around the hotel. Because the hotel was located far from the main road, and because a natural ridge followed the boundaries of the property, none of the guard towers—or other buildings on the resort for that matter—were visible to anyone on the main road.[30] Several other buildings were constructed on-site to serve as barracks, supply storage, and to service various other administrative functions.[31]

By August 29, 1942, the rapidly developing facility was re-designated with the classified designation *Camp Tracy*. Up until this point, the military had simply referred to it as *Byron Hot Springs* or *The Interrogation Center*. Furthermore, in an attempt to keep the location and JIC operations a secret, the Camp was given the more nondescript moniker of *P.O. Box 651*.[32]

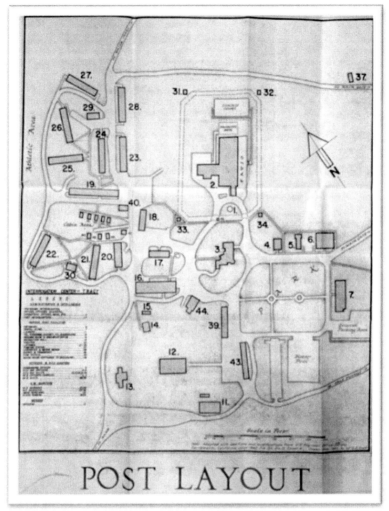

Figure 3-5: Layout of Camp Tracy.

COMMAND AND CONTROL

On May 16, 1942, by order of the Secretary of War, the JICs were designated to be under the command and control of the Army Provost Marshal General (PMG).[33] The PMG was then responsible for the appointment of commanding officers of the camps in which the JICs were located. The Camp Commanders, also known as "Post" Commanders, were charged with the daily operations of the camps, and were responsible for procuring the necessary supplies, equipment, and personnel—other than interrogators—necessary to run them.[34] The functions of the Post Commander were spelled out as follows:

> a. They will exercise jurisdiction over, and will be responsible for the post, *exclusive of the Center (Interrogation Center)* [emphasis added], including the following:
> > (1) The performance of administrative, housekeeping, and supply functions.
> > (2) He has no responsibility nor authority in connection with the commands or training of troops located at such stations, except troops of the station complement or those attached to his command for training.
> > (3) Exercise court-martial jurisdiction over all personnel.
> > (4) Be responsible for the training of Escort Guard Companies at such installations.
> > (5) *Have no control whatsoever over the part of the reservation pertaining to the Interrogation Center* [emphasis added].[35]

Because the JICs were dedicated to intelligence-gathering, they fell under the command and control of the Army Chief of Military Intelligence Service (MIS). The JIC interrogators were provided by the Army MIS and the Navy ONI and fell under the leadership of the Senior Intelligence Officer present at the camps.[36] The functions of the Senior Intelligence Officer were spelled out as follows:

> a. Responsible for the coordination of all Army and Navy activities within the Center with the Post Commanders, requesting such assistance from the Post Commander in the way of guards, messing arrangements, interrogating,

       guarding and exercising of prisoners as may be necessary.

  b. Will be responsible for the correct processing of prisoner of war mail.

  c. Is authorized to deal direct with the Chief of Military Intelligence Services, War Department, Washington D.C.[37]

Army Colonel (COL) Rhodes F. Arnold was placed in charge of Camp Tracy, while Army COL Daniel W. Kent was assigned as the Senior Intelligence Officer at the JIC.[38] While COL Arnold was in command of Camp Tracy and reported up the chain of command in traditional Army fashion, COL Kent was in charge of the JIC and reported directly to the Army Chief of MIS.

Once Camp Tracy began operations, it quickly became clear that a dual-command system was inefficient. The Army Assistant Chief of Staff for Intelligence (G-2), COL John Weckerling, soon sent a memorandum to the Commanding General of the Military District of Washington detailing the inefficiencies of the dual system; he argued, that "a unified control will result in greater efficiency and improved morale."[39] COL Weckerling's first request was denied, so he sent a second memorandum specifically requesting that a new regulation be written to place "control of joint interrogation centers in the continental United States under the Chief, Military Intelligence Service, War Department...."[40] COL Weckerling's second request was approved on April 14, 1943. Its approval resulted in the Post Commanders being reassigned to other duties, and the Senior Intelligence Officers assuming command over both the Camp and the JIC.[41]

Chapter 4

Interrogation Operations

A prisoner of war is a man who tries to kill you and fails, and then asks you not to kill him.
— **Sir Winston S. Churchill**[1]

THE INTERROGATORS

Camp Tracy was fully functional by the end of December 1942 and remained in operation until July 1945.[2] During this two-and-a-half year period over 3,500 Japanese POWs were interrogated at Camp Tracy. These interrogations resulted in more than 1,700 interrogation reports consisting of nearly 6,500 pages.[3]

A major facet of Camp Tracy's success lay in its arduous selection and assignment of interrogators. By late summer 1941, ONI and MIS had begun the process of selecting personnel to be trained as Japanese interrogators. Selection of the right type of person for the job was considered "the most important single factor in the success of an interrogation section."[4]

ONI's requirements for what it considered to be a good interrogator were very stringent:

> A good interrogator must have an adequate knowledge of the enemy's language. Complete fluency is desirable but not absolutely essential. Travel in the enemy country and a knowledge of the dialects, colloquialisms, folk lore and slang will be very useful. Ideally, he should be familiar with the national customs and superstitions of the enemy, the system of education, class or caste divisions; he should also have a background in the enemy's literature, history, geography and culture. He should be able to converse on various subjects intelligently. The ideal interrogator makes friends quickly and easily; and he must be actor enough to simulate anger or sympathy when the occasion demands.[5]

Based on these requirements, "not just anyone" could be an interrogator. Although the Navy interviewed approximately 450 prospective recruits, of them only 35 were selected for interrogation training.[6] Of those 35, five were later released because they had been found "psychologically unfit" for this sensitive and special duty.[6]

Cultural Awareness

The first Caucasian interrogators consisted mostly of men who had spent their childhood in Japan or had lived there for several years. Those who were selected as interrogators were usually the sons of missionaries, diplomats, or businessmen who had been stationed in Japan. One such Army Camp Tracy interrogator was Louis A. Nipkow, born in Japan in 1915, who was the son of a Swiss businessman working there. Nipkow spent 17 years in the country of his birth and occasionally attended parties at the

American Embassy. He then traveled to the United States and became a U.S. citizen. A few years after the beginning of WWII, Nipkow was actively recruited as an Army interrogator by COL Archibald, the former Army attaché to Japan who had been stationed at the American Embassy in Japan. COL Archibald remembered Nipkow from the Embassy parties.[8] Nipkow's linguistic knowledge and cultural expertise made him a fine candidate for interrogation operations.

Courtesy of Steve Nipkow.

Figure 4-1: U.S. Army Lieutenant Louis A. Nipkow.

Another Camp Tracy veteran interrogator was William P. Woodard, who was born in 1896 and traveled to Japan in 1921. Woodard spent three years learning Japanese in Sapporo, Japan, then worked another seventeen years in Japan and Korea as a missionary.[9] Woodard eventually returned to the United States in 1941, joined the Navy as an intelligence officer, and served as an interrogator at both Camp Tracy and Fort Hunt during WWII.[10] His detailed understanding of the Japanese vernacular and Japanese mores provided him with a solid background to excel not only at interrogation operations, but to teach the intricacies of the Japanese language and culture to other interrogators as well.[11]

Courtesy of the Special Collections & University Archives, University of Oregon Libraries.
Figure 4-2: A Young U.S. Navy Lieutenant William P. Woodard at Age 21.

A third man who illustrates the high caliber of personnel at Camp Tracy was David W. Swift Sr., born in Japan in 1896, who was the son of an American who taught at the Tokyo Imperial University.[12]   Swift lived in Japan until 1913 when he returned to the United States to attend high school and university. Following WWI, where he earned a reserve commission in the Navy, he returned to the Far East and spent another 11 years working in Japan and China for Standard Oil Company of New York.[13]

Courtesy of David W. Swift Jr..
Figure 4-3: U.S. Army Major David W. Swift Sr..

Swift transferred his reserve commission to the Army in 1933 and was brought onto active duty following the Japanese surprise attack on Pearl Harbor on December 7, 1941.[14] Prior to arriving at Camp Tracy, Swift had been assigned to General Douglas MacArthur's headquarters in Australia under Major General Charles Willoughby, MacArthur's G-2, and had commanded the American contingent of the Allied Translator and Interpreter Section.[15] Swift was pulled from this assignment and sent to Camp Tracy where, due to his extensive Japanese background and prior intelligence training, he served as the Army Senior Intelligence Officer.[16]

Training

Upon meeting the criteria for selection, the recruits were sent through intense language and interrogation training. Army personnel attended the University of Michigan for one year of in-depth Japanese language classes taught by American Nisei instructors.[17] Later in the war, Army personnel attended language training at the Military Intelligence Service Language School (MISLS), Camp Savage, Minnesota.[18] Navy personnel attended the University of Colorado for 14 months of rigorous Japanese language classes taught by American Issei and Nisei instructors.[19] Along with instruction in the Japanese language, both Army and Navy personnel were also immersed in Japanese culture and history to further their knowledge of the Japanese prisoners whom they would be interrogating.[20]

Following their rigorous language instruction, Army personnel received six months of intelligence training at the Military Intelligence Training Center (MITC) at Camp Ritchie, Maryland.[21] This consisted of general as well as specialized training which included interrogation.[22]   Upon completion of their language instruction, Navy personnel received one month of specialized intelligence training, which included interrogation, at the Henry Hudson Hotel in Manhattan, New York.[23]

An interrogator's training did not stop when he reached Camp Tracy. In addition to their normal duties conducting interrogations, transcribing POWs' conversations in the "M" room, and translating captured Japanese documents, Camp Tracy interrogators continued to refine their understanding of the Japanese language, culture, and interrogation techniques. When not conducting interrogations or assigned to some other specific duty, Camp Tracy interrogators followed this general schedule:

Daily
0800 – 1015   Reading Documents, reports, reference material, etc.
1015 – 1145   Conversation Class.

Mon/Wed/Fri
1300 – 1400   Conference periods on words, idioms, kanji.
1400 – 1630   Study on Japanese language.

Tue/Thr/Sat
1300 – 1500   Listening to records for transcription, criticism, etc.
1500 – 1630   Study on Japanese language.

Evenings
Lectures and conferences as required.[24]

THE PRISONERS OF WAR

Because of their intensive mutual animosity and the brutal fighting in which American and Japanese soldiers engaged, not many Japanese soldiers were captured. Additionally, the Japanese had a policy which forbade its servicemen from being taken prisoner for any reason.[25] The Japanese viewed being taken prisoner as a disgrace and dishonor. It was better to fight to the death, in the name of the Emperor, than be captured or to take one's own life if capture was imminent. As a result, some of the bloodiest battles in WWII occurred in the Pacific Theater against the Japanese.

For example, of the estimated 5,000 Japanese soldiers who defended the island of Tarawa against the U.S. Marines in November 1943, only seventeen survived.[26] Furthermore, of the estimated 21,000 Japanese soldiers and sailors who defended the island of Iwo Jima, only 216 survived.[27] In total, the Allied forces of the United States, Australia, New Zealand, and the United Kingdom had captured only 38,666 Japanese servicemen by the time Japan surrendered.[28] Considering the fact that Japan lost approximately 1,550,000 servicemen during WWII, the percentage of Japanese captured instead of killed amounts to only 2.5 percent.[29] These prisoners were initially sent to POW camps in the Pacific, the largest of the camps located in Australia, though in some cases POWs captured after naval battles were shipped directly to the United States.[30] One of the unintended positive results of such heavy fighting, and therefore lack of POWs, was to allow the United States the time to identify and train interrogators. This meant that later in the Pacific campaign, when more Japanese were taken prisoner, there were interrogators ready to educe information from them.

Pre-Screening

Information gleaned from the interrogations of POWs falls into two categories. The first is tactical intelligence, also known as combat intelligence, which relates directly to the composition, disposition, and intent of the enemy's tactical force. Because this information is time-sensitive and perishable, it must be harvested from a POW as quickly as possible if it is to be of use in a tactical engagement. The second category of information is strategic intelligence.[31] This is higher-level information that relates to an enemy's ability to conduct war; it includes:

> technical and scientific subjects, war economy, industrial development, civilian morale, organization of the high command, espionage and counterespionage, and the organization of railways and highways for military transport.[32]

The POW camps in the Pacific Theater served as a pre-screening location for Camp Tracy and its strategic interrogation mission. These in-theater camps were periodically updated on the types of information required for the strategic collection mission and the type of POW who was likely to have such information. POWs who met these qualifications, or who were believed to possess information on strategic-level subjects, were immediately shipped back to the United States for further interrogation at Camp Tracy.[33] For this reason, only 5,431 Japanese POWs out of the total population of over 38,000 Japanese POWs—roughly fourteen percent—were actually sent to the continental United States.[34]

Screening

Once they had arrived in the continental United States, Japanese POWs were again screened at Angel Island, their port of debarkation, just outside of San Francisco.

IMMIGRATION STATION, ANGEL ISLAND
SAN FRANCISCO BAY, CALIF.

Courtesy of Carol Jensen.
Figure 4-4: Angel Island POW Screening Facility.

Camp Tracy routinely sent interrogators to Angel Island to screen new Japanese POWs to determine which ones would be transferred to Camp Tracy for further questioning.[35] The Camp Tracy interrogators screened the POWs based on priority lists sent to them from the Army Chief of Military Intelligence Service's office via a teletype machine that had an attached scrambler device to enable secure communications (see Appendix A for a sample strategic-level questionnaire sent to Camp Tracy for use during interrogations).[36] The remaining Japanese POWs were sent to two main POW camps—Camp McCoy in Wisconsin and Camp Clarinda in Iowa.[37]

Of the 5,431 Japanese POWs transferred to the continental United States, only a few more than 3,500 were selected for interrogation at Camp Tracy.[38] Since Camp Tracy could only house 44 POWs at a time, the POWs waiting to be sent to Camp Tracy were sent to Camp Stoneman—40 miles northeast of San Francisco and 20 miles northwest from Camp Tracy—to segregate them from the main POW population being sent to the permanent Camps.[39] POWs were sent to Camp Stoneman because Angel Island could not properly segregate POW populations.[40] This segregation was necessary to prevent any collusion between the two groups of POWs.[41]

National Archives and Records Administration.
Figure 4-5: Camp Stoneman POW Holding Facility.

Processing

The POWs traveled from Camp Stoneman to Camp Tracy in a school bus with windows which had been blacked-out for security reasons.[42] No one outside the vehicle could tell that it contained Japanese POWs, and this ensured the security of the prisoners. It also guaranteed that the POWs themselves did not know where they were headed or the JIC's geographic location.

Figure 4-6: Blacked-out Bus for POW Transport.

Once they had arrived at Camp Tracy, the POWs were transferred from the vehicle directly to the receiving, or in-processing room, on the ground floor of the JIC. Any items found—"down to the smallest scrap of paper"—were collected, identified, and recorded, and a receipt for these items was given to the POW.[43] The POW was then asked some basic questions that were used by the interrogator to fill out a registration form.[44] After this in-processing had been completed, the POW was given a medical examination and once found medically fit was assigned to his living quarters on the third floor.

All items taken from the POW were added to the POW's information packet. This packet consisted of two kinds of materials: "all records on hand or received of the personnel, photos, papers with descriptions of personal effects"; and "background information taken from letters from and to the prisoners, or information received from allied sources" that had arrived with the POW.[45] These information packets, along with the registration form, were given to the interrogators to help them develop their interrogation plan.

THE INTERROGATIONS

From the moment they arrived at Camp Tracy, POWs were under observation by the interrogators so they could formulate an individually customized interrogation-approach plan of attack. The interrogators knew that time was against them with respect to the POW's attitude towards his capture. After being transferred and processed, "prisoners are uncertain of their fate, more bewildered and uncertain regarding their companions and less security conscious than they may be after becoming 'settled' in their new environment."[46] Therefore, interrogators were instructed to "look for the weaker ones," and "get these first."[47]

Planning

Interrogators spent approximately three hours preparing for every hour of actual interrogation.[48] Besides utilizing the information in the POW's information packet, the interrogators would look to other relevant sources of material to create an interrogation plan. They consulted records concerning the disposition and composition of the POW's unit, utilized intelligence reports on other POWs from the same or a similar unit, and also listened in on the POW's conversations to design each POW's individualized plan.[49]

After the interrogator had developed an approach plan and after he had checked with the "M" room to ensure that the POW was not having an intelligence-related conversation with his POW roommate, the POW would be brought downstairs to an interrogation room.[50] In the event the POW was engaged in intelligence-relevant conversation, the interrogator would either actively monitor the conversation, or read a transcript of the conversation; usually he read the transcript of the conversation because of the intensive demands on the interrogator's time. He would incorporate the new information into his interrogation-approach plan and then conduct the actual interrogation.[51]

Direct Interrogation

Camp Tracy intelligence officers found it impossible to prescribe any specific or rigid procedures for the manner in which POWs were interrogated. The major reason for this lack of uniformity in interrogation plans was that each interrogation was based on the personality of the POW, as well as the personality and skill of the interrogator, so each interrogation was different. However, Camp Tracy did impose some baseline procedures on interrogation operations to facilitate their success.

The first of these involved the guard. The guard led the POW into the interrogation room and saluted the senior interrogator, then left the room and shut the door behind him. The guard then stood post outside the room and prevented anyone, no matter what his rank or position, from entering the room while the interrogation was in process. This established an atmosphere of the all-encompassing power of the interrogators within the interrogation room; their authority was absolute.[52] Interrogators were warned, however, not to allow this sense of authority to cloud their judgment. Specifically, interrogators could "never make a promise or a threat [to a POW] that cannot be carried out according to the expectations of the prisoner."[53]

The second common procedural aspect of the interrogation involved its level of formality. Japanese POWs were required to bow to the senior interrogator and then remain at the stiff military position of attention. It was up to the senior interrogator whether the POW would remain in this pose throughout the entire interrogation session. If he felt that softening the atmosphere, and injecting a level of kindness and friendliness—such as allowing the POW to sit, or offering a cigarette or a drink—would help induce the POW to be more cooperative, it was within his authority to do so.[54]

The third procedural prescription was the utilization of two interrogators in each interrogation, one a Caucasian wearing either an Army or Navy military uniform, and the other a Nisei in civilian clothes.[55] The POWs were usually surprised to see the civilian-clothed Nisei, whom the POWs mistakenly thought were Japanese citizens.[56] Both participated in the conduct of the interrogation, which differed with each POW. In some cases, the Caucasian military officer would conduct the interrogation in English, assisted by the Nisei acting as a translator. In other cases, the Nisei would conduct the interrogation in Japanese, occasionally translating an item of information for the Caucasian military officer, who in turn would record the information in writing. During this type of interrogation the Caucasian military officer, who had received

Japanese language training, would be careful not to "let on" that he understood Japanese. This allowed the POW to talk "freely" with his fellow civilian "Japanese citizen."[57]

Camp Tracy interrogators had been instructed that "every advantage must be recognized and used at the proper time to break down, weaken, and destroy" any reluctance of the POW or measure of security-mindedness to gain the information the POW possessed.[58] Camp Tracy interrogators found that, when they utilized Nisei, they could almost always create an instant sense of rapport between the interrogators and the Japanese POWs. The phenomenon of rapport, created by the Nisei, eased the POW's resistance to questioning, facilitating the extraction of information, and served as a great advantage in the interrogation process.[59]

The fourth common procedure was the early introduction of the POW's registration form during the interrogation. Interrogators would ask questions based on the information already provided in this form by the POW, while the form itself sat within plain sight on the interrogator's desk. Camp Tracy interrogators found that this generated an atmosphere of mental domination, as the POW realized that all of his answers would be compared to information he had already provided. The interrogator typically continued with questions about the circumstances of the POW's capture. Few POWs had qualms about answering these types of questions because they felt the Americans already knew the answers. The interrogator would then subtly shift the direction of the interrogation into lines of intelligence-producing questions.[60]

This is the point where every interrogation became unique: some POWs would continue to answer questions freely and had been effectively "broken."[61] Interrogators found that other POWs, who were more reserved and not answering questions freely, were generally impressed with the amount of information interrogators already possessed, especially about the POW's unit, and about his comrades and other people with whom he was associated. Interrogators found that communication of such information tended to startle the POW and shake his confidence. Interrogators were instructed that "the best excuse for asking a question is to give the impression that you already know the answer."[62]

The "we know all" approach proved very successful in "breaking" POWs. Ulrich Straus relates in his book, *The Anguish of Surrender: Japanese POWs of World War II*, that this was the case with Ishii Shuji, a Japanese medic captured on Iwo Jima. Straus notes that in Ishii's published memoirs about his time at Camp Tracy, *Iwo-to ni ikiru* (Alive on Iwo Jima), Ishii relates that there was no reason not to answer the interrogator's questions, since the interrogators knew all of the answers anyway.[63] In this manner, Ishii and countless other POWs like him, rationalized away any hesitation or mental reservations, and answered all of their interrogator's questions.[64]

Another approach that produced a great success in "breaking" POWs was the threat to forward the POW's name and status to his relatives in Japan. To the POW, the fear of his family's learning about his capture and disgrace was a fate worse than death. Interrogators found that the "prisoner who was truculent and uncooperative" quickly became "docile and cooperative" after being threatened with having his name sent back to Japan.[65] Though this approach was highly successful when used, interrogators seldom were forced to resort to it, instead relying on other approaches to "break" the POW.[66]

The one approach Camp Tracy interrogators did not use was torture or "physical coercion." Camp Tracy interrogators understood that the threat of violence had no effect on the Japanese POW; instead, it would serve to strengthen his patriotism and resolve to die with honor for his Emperor and his country. All surviving veterans from Camp Tracy unequivocally stated that no physical coercion or violent measures were ever undertaken in an attempt to "break" a POW. Former Navy Ensign and Camp Tracy interrogator George E. Mendenhall emphasized that "coercion or torture would have been absolutely of no use, and even counter-productive."[67] Furthermore, no documentation from the U.S. National Archives, or from any published Japanese POW books or memoirs, mention the usage of physical coercion.[68]

Instead of this proscribed approach, interrogators used courtesy and kindness to conquer Japanese reluctance: they simply treated POWs as human beings. In *The Anguish of Surrender*, Straus illustrates it was this politeness and courtesy extended to Nakajima Yoshio, a Japanese artilleryman captured on Iwo Jima, by his American interrogator, which produced the answers the interrogator wanted. Straus notes that in Nakajima's book, *Iwojima*, Nakajima explains that he was amazed at the level of politeness and courtesy afforded to him by his American interrogator, a Mr. "Coleman."[69] Nakajima explains that he had intended to be uncooperative and not answer any of Mr. Coleman's questions, but he found himself answering every one. Nakajima felt that his low morale, combined with Mr. Coleman's polite and gentlemanly demeanor, overcame his resistance.[70]

Interrogations typically lasted one-to-two hours, and POWs usually had three to four interrogation sessions over a two-to-three-week period before being released for transport to one of the permanent POW camps.[71] The breaks in the interrogation sessions allowed the interrogators to review the information gathered from the POW, and to determine its veracity. The breaks also allowed interrogators to examine the information to determine what additional areas of interest the POW might possess for future interrogation sessions. Finally, interrogations were just as mentally draining on the interrogator as they were on the POW. By ending the session at a time of his choosing, the interrogator prevented his fatigue from causing any mistakes that might have alienated the POW or might have caused him to become uncooperative. The interrogator's ending of the session at his discretion also reinforced his authority and perceived power over the POW, which in turn made subsequent interrogations that much easier.[72]

Indirect Examination

In addition to direct interrogations, Camp Tracy interrogators used three other methods to garner information from the POWs: monitoring the POW living quarters to listen to their private conversations, employing "Stool Pigeons," and inspecting a POW's letters and correspondence. While these methods were not the preferred means of obtaining information, they did serve to verify information received during direct interrogation. They also provided additional information to the interrogators to further tailor their interrogation approaches.[73]

Monitoring. Camp Tracy interrogators found that POWs usually talked about their interrogation session to their POW roommate immediately upon returning to their room. This was an opportune time to monitor the POW, and it was a standing protocol to record such conversations.[74] The POW repeated the questions the interrogator had asked, and in most cases revealed the desired information to his roommate as he explained how he had "outsmarted" and "misled" the interrogator.[75]

Interrogators found further that the hours immediately following the first meeting of new roommates provided valuable collection opportunities. During this time, the POWs tended to discuss their military backgrounds and exchange information concerning their interrogation sessions. The information emerging from this "first meeting" allowed interrogators to better construct interrogation approaches for the newly arrived POW, and it also served as a control to verify the veracity of information provided by the old POW. As summarized in a Camp Tracy interrogation-information brief:

> They are, however, likely to throw a very valuable light on whether the prisoners have been telling the truth during the interrogation or whether they have attempted to lead the Interrogator astray or to withhold information. If listening in to their conversation serves not [*sic*] other purpose than this, it is worthwhile.[76]

In keeping with the intelligence-producing value of this association, POWs would occasionally be moved from one set of quarters to another to place them with new roommates. It was imperative, however, that such changes be undertaken in a way that did not invite suspicion. The interrogators were required to "keep the identity and the companions and movements of all prisoners charted for reference," and "under no conditions should 'M' room revelations be used on the prisoner unless duly covered up in a manner which is explainable to the prisoner," so as not to tip-off the POWs that their conversations were being monitored.[77]

"Stool Pigeons". Another means of eliciting information from POWs in an indirect way was the use of "Stool Pigeons," a strategy that was particularly productive when combined with the use of listening devices. It successfully generated information from the most security-conscious POW. "Stool Pigeons" were POWs who had been "turned" against their own country and who had been tasked by American intelligence officers with obtaining specific information from their fellow POWs.[78]

The selection of a POW to function in this capacity was undertaken with great caution, since the POW was in fact being asked to betray his country, Emperor, and fellow POWs. Intelligence personnel therefore carefully screened and thoroughly vetted prospective "Stool Pigeons," since the individual selected "must be thoroughly reliable, a quality normally not to be expected of men who are willing to perform this degrading function."[79] The individual also had to be a good actor because he would be playing a "role" tailored for him to get information from specifically targeted POWs. Furthermore, he must appear entirely Japanese, in appearance, manner, and language. Above all, he had to be quick-witted, and he had to have "a retentive memory and versatile conversational powers" to execute his own "interrogation operation."[80]

"Stool Pigeons" were employed in a variety of ways. Since Camp Tracy housed two POWs to a room, a "Stool Pigeon" in some cases served as a roommate for newly arrived POW, and lived with him for a certain length of time gathering information. In other cases the "Stool Pigeon" would pose as a newly arrived POW and be placed in a room with a POW who had resisted direct interrogation; he would then garner intelligence from the resistant POW, as well as any information that interrogators could use to further direct the interrogation sessions of that POW. Finally, a "Stool Pigeon" was occasionally inserted into the exercise yard to approach and befriend "obstinate prisoners" when POWs were enjoying outside time.[81]

Although "Stool Pigeons" proved very valuable in steering POW conversations along lines of intelligence interest, Camp Tracy interrogators found that the dangers involved in employing them in most cases outweighed their potential intelligence value. Their selection required great care, and selected POWs had to exercise great caution during the execution of their duties. Accordingly, "Stool Pigeons" were only infrequently utilized as an intelligence-gathering method at Camp Tracy.[82]

Written Correspondence. The final means of indirect examination was inspection of any POW-written documents. Intelligence personnel found that the Japanese seemed to have a "mania for putting things down on paper," and that they "practice writing whenever given paper and pencil."[83] Camp Tracy personnel facilitated this method of information collection by providing paper and writing materials to all POWs as soon as possible after their in-processing, so they could write while in their rooms.[84] The interrogators then, while the POWs were in the exercise yard, or in an interrogation session, conducted a sweep of the rooms, collecting and copying the written materials, and replacing them before the POWs returned to their rooms. The writings would then be translated and examined for intelligence purposes.

Camp Tracy personnel found these documents helped them gauge the mental status and personality of the POW more effectively. This added insight provided the interrogator with more information that helped him better tailor his direct interrogation approach to "break" the POW. Camp Tracy personnel also used these written materials to measure the POW's morale, a subject of strategic interest to the U.S. war effort.[85]

Reports

Following the session with the POW, interrogators faced the onerous task of preparing the interrogation report (see Appendix B for the official Camp Tracy approved format for Interrogation Reports). The level of detail and the complexity of the report depended on the amount of viable intelligence produced during the interrogation. The reporting consisted of three levels:

a. A report prepared from memory or by using interrogation notes.
b. A detailed report prepared by augmenting memory and notes with reviewing "M" room recordings of the interrogation.
c. A detailed report including a full transcription of "M" room interrogation recordings.[86]

Regardless of the level of detail, the interrogation report had a rigid format and covered the following areas:[87]

Estimate of P/W's personality.[88]
Military History and Background of P/W.
Outline of Topics covered in Interrogation.
Specific Information, such as proper names, localities.
Technical details should be included as fully as possible.
Special points of interest for monitoring.
Suggested lines for further interrogation.

These reports were used to update the files and folders on Japanese military units and records. Any significant answers or updates to previous priority intelligence requirements were then passed on to the relevant military official or department head.[90] These reports also allowed interrogators to follow up on information gained from other interrogations, and by other sources, and served as a means of double-checking overall information accuracy. As one Camp Tracy report noted, "one in two or three prisoners provided information that showed discrepancies relative to previous interrogations or otherwise known information. Generally, information became more reliable over time at the hands of skilled Nisei and Caucasian interrogators."[91]

THE INTELLIGENCE PRODUCT

Although the interrogation procedures utilized to acquire information from the Japanese POWs sent to Camp Tracy are well-documented and instructive, a direct and conclusive determination of the value of the information obtained from the sessions conducted there presents some problems. An exhaustive search of records at the National Archive and Records Administration provides no comprehensive list of items of intelligence value derived from Camp Tracy POW interrogations. However, there is indirect evidence from several sources that they did in fact provide valuable intelligence in the conduct of military operations in the Pacific.

In July 1946, Major General Clayton Bissell, Chief of the MIS, remarked at a MISLS graduation ceremony, "The magnificent work of the graduates of the Military Intelligence Service Language School in the field has been seen by your fellow Americans."[92] Furthermore, Straus lists, in *The Anguish of Surrender*, several examples of Camp Tracy intelligence coups. Items of intelligence value included information on Japanese biological weapons, new Japanese "super-battleships," code names for Japanese army units, and specifications of Japanese naval vessels.[93]

Additionally, while the archives yielded no comprehensive list of valuable intelligence items produced by the POW sessions, several individual interrogation reports located there provide some examples of the strategic-level information produced at Camp Tracy. One of the most detailed of these documents is the interrogation of Petty Officer Second Class Eikichi Saito (see Appendix C for Saito's complete interrogation packet). The information gleaned from Saito includes sketches and detailed descriptions of Japanese naval airbases, Japanese Army and Navy unit order of battle information, precise specifications of Japanese medium bomber aircraft, and evaluations of Japanese soldiers' morale.[94]

Chapter 5

Findings

The necessity of procuring good intelligence is
apparent and need not be further urged.
—**General George Washington, Commander-in-Chief,**
July 26, 1777[1]

This study first identified two important national security problems the United States currently faces: (1) the crucial need for human intelligence in the struggle for victory in the Global War on Terror; and (2) the stigma associated with coercive interrogation techniques, justified by some within the U.S. government as necessary to win the GWOT, that precipitated actual and alleged abuses against detainees in U.S. custody. In seeking ways to understand and overcome these problems, the author of this study noted parallels between the Japanese foe the United States faced in the Pacific Theater during WWII and the radical Islamists the United States currently faces in the GWOT.

Like today's radical Islamists, the Japanese enemy of over sixty years ago represented an alien, seemingly impenetrable warrior culture; they spoke an unfamiliar and complicated language, and were so fanatically committed to their cause that suicide was an acceptable and even sacred operational tactic. Yet, even when confronting such an adversary, the United States prevailed against the Japanese Empire, in part because it developed effective strategic interrogation techniques for the collection of valuable intelligence from captured Japanese POWs. If such intelligence-gathering was possible against the implacable Japanese, why is the United States having so much trouble doing the same against today's jihadists?

This quandary led to the following question: *What lessons can be learned from the experience of Camp Tracy, a U.S. strategic interrogation center for Japanese Prisoners of War during WWII, which can influence existing and future U.S. interrogation policies, doctrine, and practices?* By examining Camp Tracy, its operations and personnel, this book highlighted the methods and procedures used successfully to interrogate WWII Japanese soldiers.

The findings from this in-depth case study of Camp Tracy have direct bearing on achieving success in current and future U.S. interrogation operations in the GWOT. Not surprisingly, given the topic in question, these findings fall naturally into three categories: *policies*, *doctrine*, and *practices*.

Policies

Absolute Secrecy. The author's exhaustive search of the U.S. National Archives failed to uncover any photographs of Camp Tracy or its operations. Similarly, none of the surviving Camp

Tracy veterans had in their possession, nor could indicate the location of, any photographs or drawings of Camp Tracy. This dearth of visual evidence is directly attributable to the U.S. military's strict adherence to the security and secrecy that cloaked Camp Tracy and its operations from both the American public and the world at large. While locals in the Byron area knew about Camp Tracy's existence, they mistakenly believed it was a German and Italian POW camp. They knew nothing about the Japanese POWs who had been brought to Camp Tracy, and they knew nothing about its interrogation mission. In fact, not until fifty years after the closure of Camp Tracy's operations did the public learn of the valuable and important intelligence-gathering mission that had occurred there during WWII.

Such absolute secrecy allowed interrogators to conduct their mission without outside scrutiny. It also provided POWs with the relative assurance that the information they disclosed—in effect betrayals of their country—would remain private. Furthermore, this absolute secrecy augmented the interrogators' ability to educe information from the POWs since they suffered no additional dishonor and no disgrace.

Single Chain of Command. Camp Tracy's administrators quickly learned that a dual chain of command at a JIC was unsupportable. By consolidating command and control of the entire operation under one authority—instead of having one chain of command for the Camp, and a second chain of command for the JIC itself—Camp Tracy streamlined its operations. It was consequently better able to coordinate the movement, processing, and security of the POWs, and to thereby make the interrogation operation seamless. This in turn worked to the interrogator's advantage in several key ways: it overwhelmed the POW with the JIC's high level of efficiency and precision, and it made the POWs feel insignificant, weakening their resistance and making them more pliable to the interrogators' approaches.

Doctrine

Pre-Screening. The pre-screening of Japanese POWs, both in-theater and upon their arrival in the United States, assured that only those POWs who possessed strategic-level information were sent to Camp Tracy. In this manner, the POW "wheat" was separated from the "chaff," and Camp Tracy interrogators' valuable time and energies were not wasted on non-intelligence producing POWs. This pre-screening further allowed Camp Tracy interrogators to devote more time and effort to tailoring approaches to individual POWs, which improved the likelihood that the POWs would cooperate with the interrogators.

Interrogator Screening. ONI felt that the selection of an interrogator was "the most important single factor in the success of an interrogation section."[2] Accordingly, stringent screening criteria were devised, and only *six percent* of the personnel interviewed to become interrogators at Camp Tracy were actually selected.[3] The implementation of these criteria at Camp Tracy indicates that the selection of prospective strategic interrogators required the same careful consideration as the selection of the POWs who were actually interrogated.

Cultural Awareness. The majority of the Camp Tracy Caucasian interrogators were men who had spent many years in

Japan. Due to their complete cultural immersion, these men understood not only the Japanese language, but Japanese customs and mores as well. This understanding provided them with invaluable insight into the motivations and thought processes of the Japanese POWs. This insight, in turn, allowed them to devise their interrogation approaches in a way best-suited to gain the POWs' cooperation.

Use of Nisei. Camp Tracy interrogators found that the use of Nisei in the interrogation process built an almost instant sense of rapport between the interrogators and the POWs. The Nisei's linguistic ability were far superior to that of the Caucasian interrogators, even with their in-country experience, because of the Nisei's heritage and upbringing. The Nisei also looked Japanese, and this led some POWs to think that they were actual Japanese citizens. This shared ethnicity appears to have facilitated the extraction of information. The Nisei's complete knowledge of Japanese culture and psychology also served them well in devising interrogation approaches to gain the POWs' cooperation.

Team Concept. Camp Tracy interrogators found that the use of interrogator teams was extremely effective in obtaining the POWs' cooperation. These teams consisted of a Caucasian and a Nisei working together to educe information from the POW. This approach combined the cultural awareness of the Caucasian interrogators, and the Japanese heritage and physical racial characteristics of the Nisei, into one highly successful interrogation package. This type of teamwork allowed the Caucasian interrogator to feign ignorance of the Japanese language and listen to the POW talking freely to his fellow "Japanese citizen," the Nisei interrogator. Because of this relative freedom to speak openly, the POW provided much more information, both directly and indirectly, than would otherwise have been the case.

Practices

Preparation. Due to the multiple screenings of the POWs selected for interrogation at Camp Tracy, a substantial amount of information about each POW became available. This accumulated information provided ample material for Camp Tracy interrogators in the preparation of their interrogation approaches. Additionally, unlike the tactical environment, where time is of crucial importance in the production of combat intelligence, a strategic environment like the one at Camp Tracy provided the interrogators more latitude and flexibility. They were allowed the time, spending approximately three hours in preparation for each hour of actual interrogation, to review all information concerning the POW; they could also listen in on the POW himself, and this in turn aided them in devising successful interrogation approaches to elicit the POW's cooperation.[4]

Power over POW. The entire Camp Tracy interrogation process, from the POW's arrival at the camp to his eventual departure, was designed to overwhelm the POW and degrade his capacity to resist questioning. From the time he arrived, the POW was told what to wear, when he would rise in the morning, when he would go to sleep, when and what he would eat, and when he would be allowed outside. The POW had no control over what room he lived in, how often he was moved, who his roommates were, and how often he was brought to the interrogation room.

The power of Camp Tracy was purposefully vested in the POW's interrogator. To the POW, this was the man that the guards saluted and to whom they were obedient. This was the man who could provide, or take away, all of the POW's amenities. This was the man who seemed to already know everything about him. This perceived power that the POW ascribed to the interrogator ultimately had the desired effect of psychologically "softening" the POW's resistance to the interrogator's questioning.

Courtesy/Kindness. The Camp Tracy experience shows that torture or "physical coercion" was not necessary for the successful eduction of information from POWs. In fact, quite the opposite was true: Camp Tracy interrogators found that courtesy and kindness overcame most Japanese reluctance and reticence. The experience of Nakajima Yoshio as a POW interrogated at Camp Tracy, and his explanation that the courtesy he received overcame his resistance to questioning, along with the many accounts set forth by Straus in *The Anguish of Surrender*, confirm and emphasize this significant fact about the Camp Tracy interrogations.

Shame/Dishonor. Because of their cultural expertise, Camp Tracy interrogators understood that for a Japanese soldier to be captured by the enemy—instead of being killed in battle—was a great dishonor to both the individual and his family. The interrogators capitalized on this fear of dishonor by threatening to send word of the POW's capture back to his family in Japan, or conversely, by promising *not* to send the POW's name and status back to Japan. The fear of dishonoring himself and his family was so great that most POWs quickly became cooperative.

CONCLUSION

By looking to the past and determining how the United States successfully educed information from a foreign and hostile culture, we can create a blue-print to use as a starting point today. The National Archives and Records Administration contains thousands of declassified documents pertaining to WWII interrogation operations, this unparalleled primary-source research material can provide further unique insights and fresh perspectives. Additionally, oral history programs such as the U.S. Library of Congress' Veterans History Program (http://www.loc.gov/vets// vets-home.html) and the Go For Broke National Education Center's Hanashi Oral History Program (http://www.goforbroke.org) help preserve the knowledge and experience of our aging veterans and ensure their hard earned wisdom survives for the benefit of future generations.

Chapter 6

Epilogue

Following the suspension of interrogation operations and the transfer of all POWs to Fort Hunt in July 1945, Camp Tracy began the process of deactivation. As part of that process, the U.S. Army removed all specialized intelligence equipment and as many of the physical improvements made to the resort as were transportable. This "stripping" of the facilities left the resort in a state of shambles when it was returned to the owner, Mae Mead Reid. By September 1, 1945, the camp was officially ordered closed.

As for the Japanese POWs themselves, they were quickly shipped out of the continental United States, with the first groups departing less than a month after the Japanese had signed the Instrument of Surrender aboard the *USS Missouri*.[1] They were either shipped directly back to Japan, or they were sent to POW-processing facilities in the South Pacific region.

During the sixty years since the end of WWII, ownership of the Byron Hot Springs Resort has passed to several different holders, and the facility has been reinvented multiple times. Among its reincarnations it became a Greek Orthodox monastery, a private country club, and a fairground for Renaissance Faires.

Courtesy of Carol Jensen.
Figure 6-1: Byron Hot Springs Resort as a Greek Orthodox Monastery.

Tragically, in one of its most recent incarnations it became a haven for vandals and graffiti artists who destroyed the few remaining vestiges of the resort's natural beauty. In 2008 the property was purchased by a developer who intends to restore the facility as a resort destination and spa. In doing so, he will not only bring Byron Hot Springs Resort full-circle back to its original purpose, but will also preserve this significant aspect of U.S. military history for all time.

For more information about the history and future of Byron Hot Springs Resort, please visit the East Contra Costa Historical Society (http://www.theschoolbell.com/history) or the Byron Hot Springs Resort online (http://www.byronhotsprings.com/home.html).

Appendix A

Propaganda, Morale, and Related Subjects[1]

INTRODUCTION.

1.   Morale data in interrogation reports is a most important source of information concerning changes occurring behind the enemy lines. While it is true that behavior in battle is the best indicator of total morale, it is also important to know what this morale is made of and where its strong and weak points lie. This is of increasing significance in view of the fact that while Japanese morale is still very high, there are indications from many sources to show that it is not so high as it was a year ago in numbers of areas. When morale data gathered from prisoners is correlated with actual performance of various enemy units, it will be possible to have some fore-knowledge of where cracks in morale are likely to occur and to adopt military and psychological warfare measures accordingly.

2.   A unit has been established to coordinate and

analyze data on enemy morale from all theatres in the Far East. Some of the best material available is to be found in the P/W interrogation reports. However, it is felt that this could be made still better if the reports were more consistent in their treatment of subjects related to morale. Consequently, the following list of questions are suggested. It is realized that many of them are already being asked in the P/W inquires, but they are offered here as a check list. In the report, the following data on each question should be given:

      a.   Those cases in which the information was not sought.

      b.   Those cases in which it was sought and could not be obtained.

      c.   Those cases in which it was obtained but is deemed by the interviewer to be unreliable.

      d.   Those cases in which it was obtained and is deemed reliable.

      For the purposes of analysis and statistics, negative statements are as important as positive statements. Omissions always leave the analyst in doubt as to whether the material was not found, or was not reported. One hundred P/W interrogations carefully done on a random sampling basis with every question covered are more valuable than thousands in which the questioning is done on a haphazard basis.

      3. It is realized that in getting information out of Ps/W, rapport is the most important factor. In consequence, the questions which follow are not designed to be used directly, but are matters for the interviewer to have in his mind and to work out with the best method at his disposal.

      4. Many reports indicate that during the first weeks after capture is the time when Ps/W talk most freely, and that after a month or more, they are inclined to develop resistance or stereotyped answers. It is therefore most desirable to have the interviews conducted as soon after capture as practicable.

5.   As a matter of interest and possible utility, a working definition of morale is given below. This is a definition employed by the group analyzing the P/W reports.

Morale is the capacity of a group of men to pull together persistently and consistently in pursuit of a common purpose. This state depends on five general types of factors:

a.   The faith of each member of the group in the common purpose.

b.   The faith of each member of the group in the leadership.

c.   The faith of each member of the group in the other members.

d.   The organizational efficiency of the group.

e.   The health and balance of emotions in members of the group.

6.   All reports show that the investigation of morale of Japanese Ps/W is a highly complex problem, due to the very complete indoctrination which the Japanese receive from early childhood, and which is strengthened in Army life. It is doubtful if any single set of questions will alone be sufficient to secure the desired information on morale, and the points at which it can be attacked. It is strongly recommended, therefore, that at the time these questions are sent to the field, a person skilled in sociological interviewing be sent out also to give specific training to interrogators in the problems involved in the investigation of morale. Only in this way, it is believed, can data which are uniformly valuable and reliable be secured. The Sociological Branch is prepared to recommend personnel suitable for this work.

INTERROGATOR's EVALUTATION OF PRISONER.

1.   As full a picture as possible should be given of the appearance and behavior of the prisoner during the interview. What emotions does he show during the interview, or report from the period of his army services, that could reasonable be considered to show calmness, courage, and good balance? What does he report that indicates anxiety, fear, sadness, hopelessness or other states of mind which would operate against effective pulling together with the group?

2.   Intelligence of the P/W should be rated in standard form:

Dull,

Average,

Superior.

3.   Willingness to cooperate and impart information should be rated in standard form:

Uncooperative,

Moderately cooperative,

Very cooperative.

4.   Degree to which the P/W is indoctrinated with the ideals of the Japanese soldier should be rated in standard form:

Low,

Average,

Superior.

5.   Degree to which the P/W has become conditioned and "trained" in his replies by previous interviews should rated in standard form:

None,

Moderate,

Considerable.

6.   General estimate of degree of reliability of P/W's statements should be recorded in standard form:

Poor,

Average,

High.

BACKGROUND QUESTIONS. These questions, many of which are already in use, are designed to give sufficient information on the P/W to enable the analyst to interpret and evaluate his responses. They should be recorded systematically for each P/W interrogated.

1.   Name.

2.   Grade.

   a.   Time in grade.

3.   Serial number.

4.   Organization.

5.   Longevity.

   a.   In service (date of induction.)

   b.   Outside of Japan.

   c.   In last station.

6.   Duty assignment.

7.   Age.

8. Education

    a. Grade completed.

    b. Higher schools attended, by name.

    c. Ability to speak, read English.

9. Marital Status

    a. Number of children.

    b. Other dependents.

10. Civilian occupation.

11. Place of residence before induction. (Note whether rural, village, town, or large city).

12. Social class. (Note particularly whether P/W is an Eta or an Okinawan). (It will of course be noted if P/W is Formosan, Korean, or Chinese).

13. Circumstances of capture. Every effort should be made to secure verification of P/W's own statements.

PHYSICAL CONDITION. Any data bearing on physical condition of P/W and other Army Personnel should be secured.

1. How does P/W rate his own physical condition:

    a. For six months preceding capture?

    b. At time of capture?

    c. At time of interrogation?

2. Is P/W's own statement on physical condition at time of capture at variance with other reports on P/W?

3. What illnesses has P/W had since being inducted?

(List each specific illness by name, date and duration.)

4. What was physical condition of P/W's fellows for six months preceding his capture?

5. What is P/W's physical classification (by Japanese Army standards)?

a. Does P/W know if physical standards for Army (or Navy) induction have been lowered in recent months?

6. Does P/W know any cases of battle neuroses ("shell-shock")? What treatment, if any, was used for these cases?

MORALE OF MILITARY FORCES. Much of the material for this section is drawn from the attached "Outline for Guiding Inquiry into Prisoner of War Morale" (Tab B), which should be referred to for greater elaboration of several of the questions listed below.[2] Note that one of the most important problems will be to determine the extent and direction of changes in the P/W's attitudes since capture.

1. Faith of P/W in the cause.

a. Is P/W certain that Japan will win the war? What are his doubts, if any? How long will the war last?

b. Does P/W feel that right and justice are on the side of Japan? Does he personally believe in the war?

c. Does P/W believe that Japan is and should be fighting to save Asia from exploitation and domination by Western countries?

d. Is there any indication that P/W belongs to a group in Japan which he believes is not getting as much out of the war as other groups?

2. Faith of P/W in leaders.

a. Does P/W have faith in the Emperor? Does

P/W think that the Emperor would make peace with United States even though Japan had not won the way?

      b. Does P/W have faith in top political leaders? (It may be important, in this connection, to find out if P/W knows who the top political leaders are.)

      c. What is attitude of P/W toward his officers?

         (1) Were they good leaders in battle? In terms of courage? judgment? experience?

         (2) Did they show proper concern for welfare of men?

    3. <u>Faith of P/W in other members of his group</u>.

      a. Did P/W have faith in members of his own company (or comparable unit)? Does he now feel that any lack of effort or support by them was responsible for his capture? Did any of them lack fighting spirit?

      b. Did P/W have faith in the larger unit of which he was a member, for example, infantry, air force, navy, etc?

      c. Are there indications of jealousy between Army and Navy?

      d. Does P/W feel that Army (or Navy) is receiving full support of Japanese civilians? Does P/W know of any groups in Japan which do not fully support the war? Do people in Japan fully appreciate the task of the combat soldier?

    4. <u>Attitude of P/W toward foreigners</u>.

      a. Does P/W believe that Koreans are actively support ing the war? Formosans?

      b. What is attitude of P/W toward satellite countries: Manchuko, Indo-China, Burma?

c.   What is P/W's attitude toward Chinese?
Are they guilty of starting the war, or are they acting only under
pressure of the Western countries? Does P/W show animosity
toward the Chinese as individuals?

d.   What are P/W's attitudes toward the United
States, Great Britain, Russia individually? Are there differences in
attitude toward each of these countries?

e.   What does P/W think will happen to Japan
if the United States wins the war? Has his attitude in this respect
changed since his capture?

f.   How does P/W rate righting ability of
American soldiers? How does he rate American weapons? What
were the weapons he feared most?

g.   What is P/W's attitude toward populations
of occupied areas?

5.   Attitude toward organizational efficiency.

a.   Does P/W feel that every possible attempt
was made to keep him well supplied? (Note that this is a question
of intent rather than fact.)

b.   Were food supplies, pay, ammunition and
equipment generally adequate in the six months preceding the
P/W's capture?

c.   Does P/W feel that there was adequate
coordination between army, navy and air forces? (Cite examples of
lack of coordination.) Whom does P/W blame?

d.   Does P/W feel that his training was
adequate? Was that of other members of his organization? Were
replacements adequately trained? If training not adequate in any
respect, give particulars.

e.   Does P/W feel that his weapons were as

good as those of the Americans? Which were better, which poorer?

      f.   What was done by the Japanese Army to provide recreational activities for the troops (similar to Special Service in the United States Army)?

    6. <u>Capture</u>.

      a.   What reasons does P/W give for his capture?

      b.   Did he make any attempts at suicide? Does it appear that they were bona fide attempts?

      c.   Is P/W apprehensive about eventual return to Japan because of capture?

      d.   Does P/W have any suggestions as to ways of influencing others to surrender?

<u>PROPAGANDA</u>. It is desired to know whether P/W has heard U.S. radio broadcasts, has seen leaflets, or has been exposed to other U.S. propaganda, and the reaction of P/W to these activities.

    1. Did P/W's outfit have a radio to which men could listen?

    2. Did P/W hear any radio programs put out by U.S. or Allied forces?

      a.   What is P/W's attitude toward these programs? Did they influence him to surrender?

      b.   Did P/W know any men who had listened?

      c.   What was attitude of P/W's fellows toward these programs?

      d.   Were there any prohibitions against listening to foreign programs?

    3. Has P/W seen any leaflets?

a. What is P/W's attitude toward these leaflets? Did they influence him to surrender?

b. Did P/W know any other men who had seen leaflets?

c. What was attitude of P/W's fellows toward leaflets?

d. Were there any prohibitions against reading or keeping leaflets?

e. (For particularly cooperative Ps/W.) What changes in leaflets would P/W suggest to make them more effective?

4. How well informed was P/W before capture as to the extent of U.S. operations? Does P/W now feel that he had been misinformed?

SOCIAL CONDITIONS IN JAPAN (Other than Morale). It is desired, under this heading to get an estimate, insofar as the P/W can or will give information, on changes in living and working conditions in areas of Japan and the satellite areas with which P/W may be familiar. In each case there should be an indication as to whether the information is based on first-hand observation, or whether it is based on letters or hearsay.

1. When did P/W last see his family? When did P/W last receive letter from family?

2. How is P/W's family faring in the war?

a. Are their living conditions in general better or worse than they were in 1941?

b. Are they able to get enough food?

c. What specific food are they unable to get

enough of now?

        d.   Have rents increased? How much?

        e.   Have taxes increased? How much?

    3.   What are the occupations of the family? (Father, brothers, sisters.)

        a.   Have any members of the family changed their occupations since 1941? If so, what were the changes?

    4.   What is the P/W's home community?

        a.   Has the population of his home community changed much since 1941? If so, how much and why? (Indicate here any new industries, etc.)

        b.   Have any members of P/W's family changed their residence since 1941? If so, give details?

    5.   How is health of P/W's family? Have any been ill, or died, since 1941? If so, give details?

        a.   What epidemics, if any, does P/W know of?

<u>CIVILIAN MORALE</u>. If P/W has had any contact with civilians, either directly or by letter, secure all possible information on morale of the home front.

    1.   Are there any groups in Japan which do not fully support the war? Are there groups which would not want to make peace with the United States?

    2.   How long do the people of Japan think the war is going to last?

    3.   Are there any Japanese people who are afraid that the United States will win the war? Are there any who would like to see the United States win so that they would be a change in government?

4. Are there any groups which do not have confidence in the ability of the present government to carry out the war successfully?

5. If the Emperor should offer to make peace with the United States, what would be the attitude of the people?

6. <u>Effect of bombing.</u>

    a. How have the attitudes of the people of Japan been affected by the bombings? Has it made them feel that there is some possibility that Japan might lose the war? Have the bombings made people work harder, or have they made them more resigned?

    b. How does P/W feel about the bombings?

    c. What is source of P/W's information about the bombings (direct observation, letters from people in bombed areas, hearsay)? If P/W has received information direct from some one in the area, or observed it himself, secure all possible information.

Appendix B

Outline for Interrogations[1]

A. <u>Personal History Form</u>: The interrogator will complete this form during his first interrogation of the PW.

B. <u>Reports</u>: Further interrogations will continue, and reports will be prepared according to the following outline. <u>Consult current directives for special information needed</u>.

1. Preamble:

    a. Year and prefecture of PW's birth; registered domicile; education.
    b. Reference to previous interrogation reports on PW (if necessary).
    c. Assessment of reliability of PW's statements at this unit.

2. <u>Capture</u>:

      a.   When, where, agency and circumstances of capture.

3. Localities:

      a.   General.
      b.   Waterfront facilities.
      c.   Buildings.
      d.   Airdromes, landing strips, dispersal areas.
      e.   W/T, radar.
      f.   Dumps—fuel, ammunition and stores.
      g.   Defense works, minefields, etc.

4. Ships:

      a.   List information in following order: date of PW's observation, name, tonnage, construction, engine, armament, duty, when and where damaged or sunk.

          (1) Warships.
          (2) Merchant ships.

5. Aircraft:

      a.   The following interrogation will be on aircraft in which PW has actually served.

          (1) Type and model (recognitions).
          (2) Engine.
          (3) Construction.
          (4) Performance.
          (5) Markings.
          (6) Gun positions.
          (7) Arc of fire.
          (8) Bomb-load.
          (9) Fuel.
          (10)   Crew.
          (11)   Vulnerable points.
          (12)   Camouflage.
          (13)   Instruments and apparatus.
          (14)   PW's opinion of his aircraft and

equipment. Defects and deficiencies experienced in combat.

(15)   There based and how long.

(16)   Route followed from previous base to present base.

b. Other A/C (sub-headings same as above), expecially improvements and new types.

c. List of Japanese aircraft.

d. Number of aircraft operating in areas known to PW.

e. General:

(1) Airplane factories in Japan and occupied areas.

(2) Repairs on damaged planes.

(3) Octane value of fuel.

(4) Possible shortages of parts, fuel, etc.

f. New aircraft equipment: radio-controlled bombing, robot planes, etc.

6. <u>Equipment</u>:

a. Weapons and ammunition.

(1) Artillery – Field.

(2) Artillery – Mountain.

(3) Artillery – AA.

(4) Artillery – AT.

(5) Artillery – Medium;
                Heavy.

(6) Mortars.

(7) Machine guns.

(8) Small arms.

(9) Grenades.

(10)   Smoke apparatus.

(11)   Tanks.

(12)   Mines and booby traps.

(13)   Explosives.

(14)   Bombs.

(15)   Pyrotechnics.

b. Instruments and apparatus.

(1) Cameras.
(2) Optical equipment.

c. AA fire-control equipment: Position finding, height finding, data computer, fire-control equipment installed on gun, sound locator, searchlight, new tactics.
d. Radar.
e. Maps, charts and booklets.
f. Clothing.

(1) Uniforms.
(2) Personal equipment, mess kit, helmet, etc.
(3) Footwear.
(4) Flying suits, snow suits, etc.

7. <u>Enemy Methods</u>:

a. Overseas supply and evacuation.
b. Transportation.

(1) Transports and supply ships.

(a) Wooden ships.

(2) Vehicles and equipment used in transporting troops and supplies.
(3) Landing craft used by the Army.
(4) Overseas supply and evacuation.

c. Engineers.

(1) Special equipment.
(2) Bridge materials.
(3) Construction material for barracks, buildings, etc.
(4) Special transportation methods employed by Engineer Units.
(5) Repairs, methods of making.

        (6) Labor troops.

        (7) Heavy equipment for constructing roads, railroads, air-fields, etc.

8. Conscription and Mobilization:

    a. Recent changes in system (age of conscripts, age of retirement, etc).
    b. Training.
    c. Replacements.
    d. Recent changes in Army educational system.
    e. Promotion system.
    f. Pay.

9. Operational Methods: This section applies to strategical and tactical methods in the conduct of the war.

    a. Defensive position. Have PW show by chart disposition of troops, gun emplacements, ammunition dumps, barracks, etc, of all places where he was stationed; especially land and beach defensive positions; reinforcement operations.
    b. March conditions and dispositions.
    c. Tactical maneuvers.

        (1) Defensive.
        (2) Offensive.

10. Intelligence and Security:

    a. Information and reconnaissance patrols.
    b. Security patrols.
    c. Intelligence and sabotage schools.
    d. Deception.
    e. Camouflage and dummy installations.
    f. Photography.
    g. Aircraft tactics.

        (1) Number of planes assigned to mission, course planned from base to target and return, altitude and speed, details of attack.

      (2) Fighter tactics against fighters and bombers.
      (3) Bomber tactics.
      (4) Night fighters.
      (5) Air support.

11. Communications:

    a. Communications net.
    b. Radio.
    c. Telegraph and telephone.
    d. Look-outs.
    e. Post offices.
    f. Railways and tramways.
    g. Roads, tracks, bridges.
    h. Air-ground, ground-air, air-air signals.

12. Defenses:

    a. Field fortifications.
    b. Anti-tank.
    c. Mine fields.
    d. A/A, bomb shelter, protection methods, etc.

13. Enemy Supplies:

    a. Fuel oil.
    b. Gasoline.
    c. Lubricants. Daily issue, transportation in field, effect of weather on, etc.
    d. Ammunition.
    e. Provisions, stores, including rations. Proportion of food obtained locally, especially in combat areas.
    f. Ration and ration scale.
    g. Water supply (see also 18e).

14. Morale and Propaganda: Definite answers are desired on the following subjects for use in psychological warfare. (Note only unusual statements.)

    a. Views on the outcome of the present war.
    b. Attitude toward the present military regime.

    c. Attitude toward the Emperor.
    d. Feeling about home front (conditions in Japan).
    e. Views on the effectiveness of Allied raids.

      (1) On Japanese homeland.
      (2) In Theater of Operations.

    f. Attitude toward enemy nations.

      (1) General.
      (2) Toward U.S.A.
      (3) Toward China.
      (4) Toward Great Britain.

    g. Attitude toward Russia.
    h. Reactions to propaganda.

      (1) Allied leaflets.
      (2) Loud-speaker broadcast in the front line.
      (3) Allied radio broadcast.
      (4) Japanese radio broadcast.
      (5) Dissemination of information on battle losses and reactions of people and soldier casualties, shipments, etc.

    i. Post-war expectation if Japan loses.

      (1) For PW.
      (2) For the Empire.

    j. Service conditions, mail, relations between officers and men, hunger, disease, climate, mosquitoes.
    k. Fighting qualities.
    l. Japanese opinion of American weapons.
    m. Japanese opinion of American tactics.
    n. Complaints.

15. <u>Enemy Intentions</u>: (State clearly whether knowledge, rumor or opinion.)

16. <u>Wastage and Casualties</u>:

    a. General.
    b. Land.
    c. Air.

17. Chemical Warfare:

    a. General (gas units, decontamination methods, etc).
    b. Land.
    c. Air.

18. Medical:

    a. General.
    b. Hospitals.

        (1) Casualty clearing stations.
        (2) Field hospitals.
        (3) Line of Communications hospitals.
        (4) Base hospital

    c. Rest huts.
    d. Medical supplies.
    e. Hygiene and treatment (including drugs, medicines, inoculations, sanitation, water supply, etc).
    f. Incidence, types and causes of sickness.
    g. Evacuation of sick and wounded.
    h. Unethical practices.
    i. Veterinary.
    j. Biological warfare.

19. Allied Forces:

    a. General (Enemy reports on Allied losses) (See Sec. 14e, f).
    b. Captured Allied material (See Sec. 14e).

20. Special Intelligence: Information of value in economic warfare. Japan and occupied areas.

    a. Raw materials, coal, iron ore, petroleum, rubber, etc.

    b. Industries: expansion, dispersal into small communities, etc.

    c. Commercial shipping and transportation, coastwise shipping, bottoms available, weakness in system, etc.

    d. Shortages in equipment and material. Rationing, scrap iron collections—iron, steel, aluminum, etc.

    e. Labor: wages, hours, manpower supply, women in industry and agriculture.

    f. Developments of hydro-electric power, restrictions on use, etc.

    g. Black market.

    h. Industrial development in occupied areas.

    i. See "Information desired about Japanese-occupied territories."

21. <u>General</u>:

    a. Comments.

    b. Pertinent information from other sources.

    c. Activities in occupied countries.

    d. Japanese military and technical terms, symbols and abbreviations in common use in the field.

22. <u>Questionnaire</u>.

23. <u>Chronology</u>:

    a. Specialized schooling and occupations of PW.

    b. Movements of PW in homeland from date of induction.

    c. Voyage out, all places visited enroute.

    d. Movement in Theater of Operations.

24. <u>Order of Battle</u>:

    a. <u>Unit or Force</u>: List organizations in which PW served and dates.

b. Identifications: Include all organizations other than
    PW's.

   (1) Movements of all ships, especially any
       convoys, with destination and units carried.
   (2) Standard organizations.
   (3) Strength and armament.
   (4) Transportation (cf. Sec. 23c).
   (5) Unit losses (cf. Sec. 16).
   (6) Dispositions.
   (7) Code names and numbers, home and overseas
       code designations.
   (8) Defense zones.
   (9) Air organization – general.
   (10)   Air organization – Army.
   (11)   Paratroops, commandoes and all special
          units (including SNLP).
   (12)   History, movements and operations.
   (13)   Imperial General Headquarters.

c. Personalities: List in following order: rank, last
    name (alphabetically), first name, assignment, unit,
    date of PW's observation.

   (1) Army officers.
   (2) Army enlisted personnel.
   (3) Army air officers.
   (4) Army air enlisted personnel.
   (5) SNLP (and related) officers.
   (6) SNLP (and related) enlisted personnel.
   (7) Koreans, Formosans, Chinese and
       Manchurians.

25. Appendix:

   a. Translation of notes found in PW's possession.
   b. Excerpts from reports made at other units.

*****

Appendix C

The Saito
Interrogation Packet[1]

To provide readers with a more thorough understanding of the interrogation process, this Appendix follows the story of Eikichi Saito, a Petty Officer Second Class (PO 2/C) in the Japanese Navy. He was captured February 22, 1944 off the island of Kavieng, Papua New Guinea, when his ship, the NAGAURA MARU, was sunk by Allied destroyers. He was initially screened, photographed, fingerprinted, and interrogated at the South Pacific Force Combat Intelligence Center, located in Australia (see Figure C-1 through C-11).

PO 2/C Saito was then selected for strategic-level interrogation at Camp Tracy. He was transferred to the continental United States where he was further screened at Angel Island (see Figure C-12 through C-14) before being sent to Camp Tracy (see Figure C-16 and C-17).

After in-processing at Camp Tracy (see Figure C-18), Saito was interrogated from April 5 through April 10, 1944. From these sessions, Camp Tracy interrogators produced a 13-page interrogation report which included several maps based on information educed from Saito (See Figure C-21 through C-33). Saito was then transferred to a permanent POW camp.

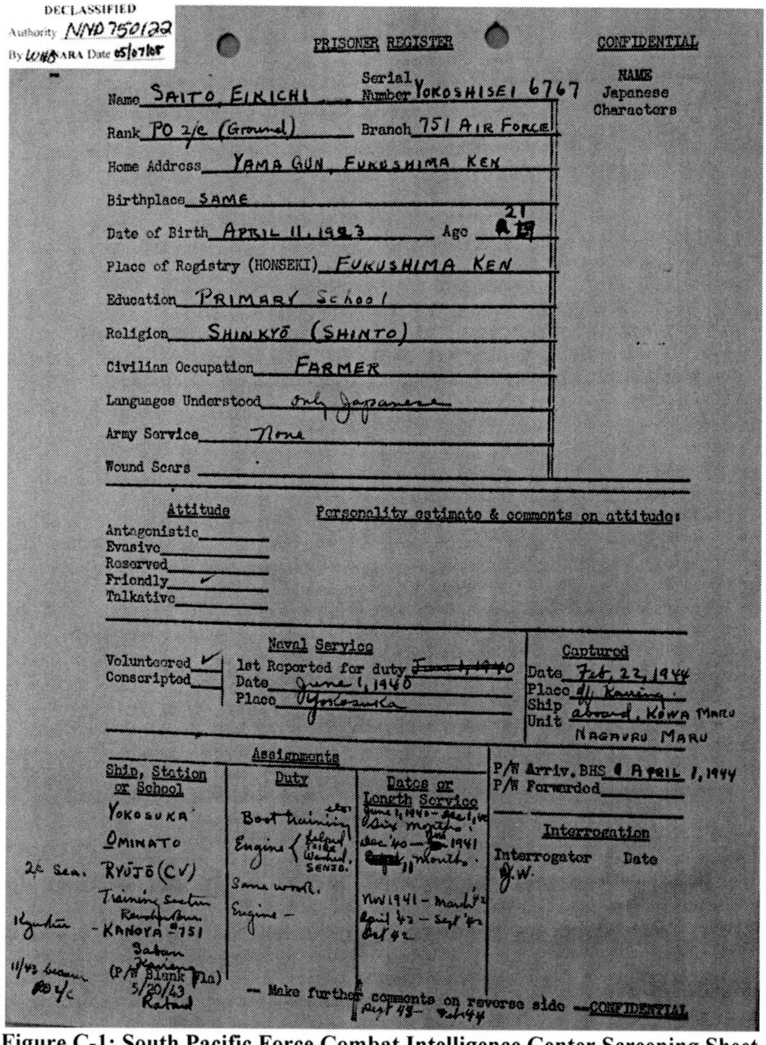

DECLASSIFIED
Authority NND 750122
By LH&ARA Date 05/07/08

PRISONER REGISTER

CONFIDENTIAL

Name SAITO, EIKICHI   Serial Number YOKOSHISEI 6767

NAME Japanese Characters

Rank PO 2/c (Ground)   Branch 751 AIR FORCE

Home Address YAMA GUN, FUKUSHIMA KEN

Birthplace SAME

Date of Birth APRIL 11, 1923   Age 21

Place of Registry (HONSEKI) FUKUSHIMA KEN

Education PRIMARY School

Religion SHINKYŌ (SHINTO)

Civilian Occupation FARMER

Languages Understood only Japanese

Army Service None

Wound Scars .

Attitude   Personality estimate & comments on attitude:
Antagonistic
Evasive
Reserved
Friendly ✓
Talkative

Naval Service
Volunteered ✓   1st Reported for duty
Conscripted   Date June 1, 1940
Place Yokosuka

Captured
Date Feb. 22, 1944
Place di Kavieng
Ship aboard, Kowa Maru
Unit Nagauru Maru

Assignments

Ship, Station or School	Duty	Dates or Length Service	
YOKOSUKA	Boot training	June 1940 - Aug '40	P/W Arriv. BHS 1 April 1, 1944
OMINATO	Engine	Dec '40 - 1941	P/W Forwarded
RYŪJŌ (CV)	Training Section	Nov 1941 - March '42	Interrogation
-KANOYA #751	Engine	April '42 - Sept '42	Interrogator Date
(P/W Blank Pla) 5/20/43		Aug '43 - Feb '44	P.W.

— Make further comments on reverse side — CONFIDENTIAL

Figure C-1: South Pacific Force Combat Intelligence Center Screening Sheet.

Screening sheets gave interrogators some basic facts about the POW that could be used as a starting point in developing the interrogation plan and help determine what type of information the POW might likely possess.

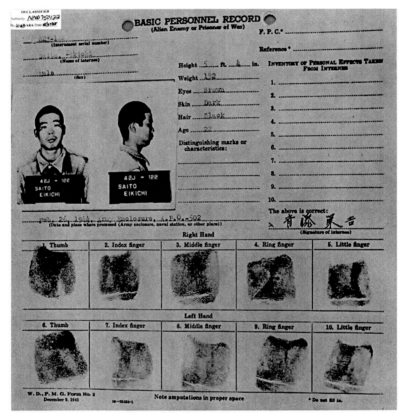

Figure C-2: Saito POW Record.

Photographs and fingerprints served to further identify the POWs and ensure an accurate management of the POWs during transportation.

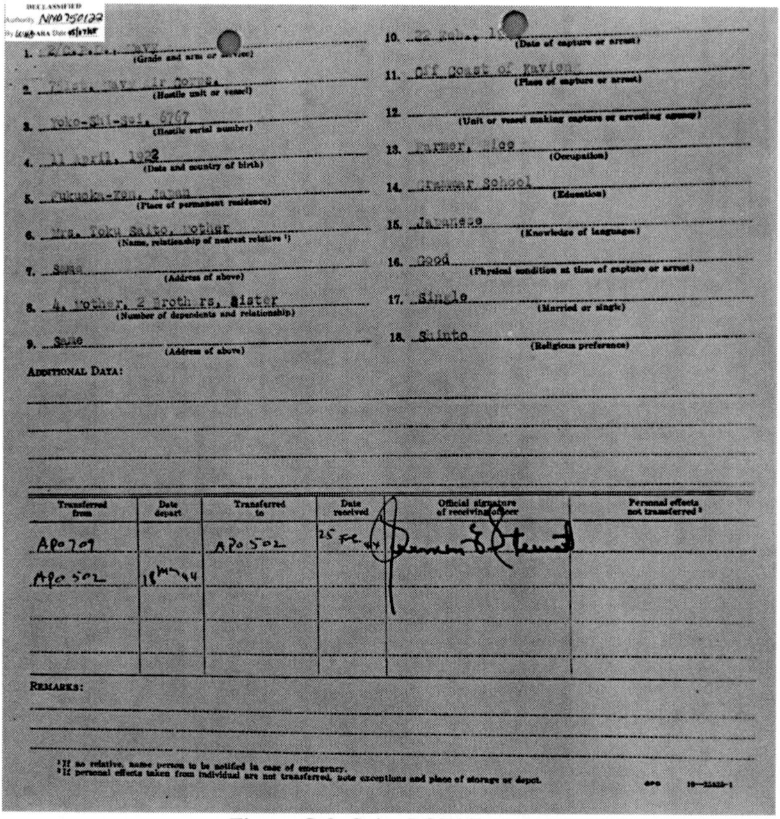

Figure C-3: Saito POW Record.

The rear side of the POW record recorded the POWs basic biographical data, capture information, and served as a record of which POW camps the POW had previously been located.

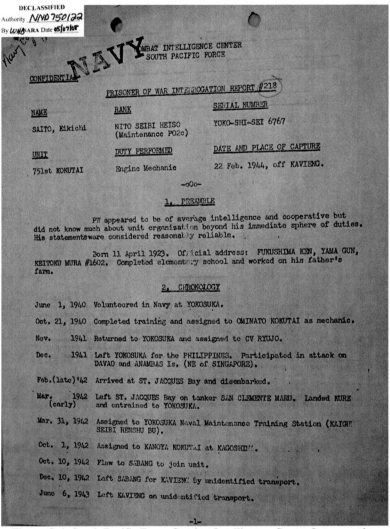

COMBAT INTELLIGENCE CENTER
SOUTH PACIFIC FORCE

CONFIDENTIAL

PRISONER OF WAR INTERROGATION REPORT #218

NAME	RANK	SERIAL NUMBER
SAITO, Eikichi	NITO SEIBI HEISO (Maintenance PO2c)	YOKO-SHI-SEI 6767

UNIT	DUTY PERFORMED	DATE AND PLACE OF CAPTURE
751st KOKUTAI	Engine Mechanic	22 Feb. 1944, off KAVIENG.

-oOo-

1. PREAMBLE

PW appeared to be of average intelligence and cooperative but did not know much about unit organization beyond his immediate sphere of duties. His statements were considered reasonably reliable.

Born 11 April 1923. Official address: FUKUSHIMA KEN, YAMA GUN, KEITOKU MURA #1602. Completed elementary school and worked on his father's farm.

2. CHRONOLOGY

June 1, 1940	Volunteered in Navy at YOKOSUKA.
Oct. 21, 1940	Completed training and assigned to OMINATO KOKUTAI as mechanic.
Nov. 1941	Returned to YOKOSUKA and assigned to CV RYUJO.
Dec. 1941	Left YOKOSUKA for the PHILIPPINES. Participated in attack on DAVAO and ANAMBAS Is. (NE of SINGAPORE).
Feb.(late) '42	Arrived at ST. JACQUES Bay and disembarked.
Mar. 1942 (early)	Left ST. JACQUES Bay on tanker SAN CLEMENTE MARU. Landed KURE and entrained to YOKOSUKA.
Mar. 31, 1942	Assigned to YOKOSUKA Naval Maintenance Training Station (KAIGUN SEIBI RENSHU BU).
Oct. 1, 1942	Assigned to KANOYA KOKUTAI at KAGOSHIMA.
Oct. 10, 1942	Flew to SABANG to join unit.
Dec. 10, 1942	Left SABANG for KAVIENG by unidentified transport.
June 6, 1943	Left KAVIENG on unidentified transport.

-1-

Figure C-4: South Pacific Force Combat Intelligence Center Interrogation Report.

Based on the information provided in this interrogation report, particularly his knowledge of Japanese morale, military airfields and the possibility of chemical warfare, PO 2/C Saito was selected for strategic-level interrogation in the United States.

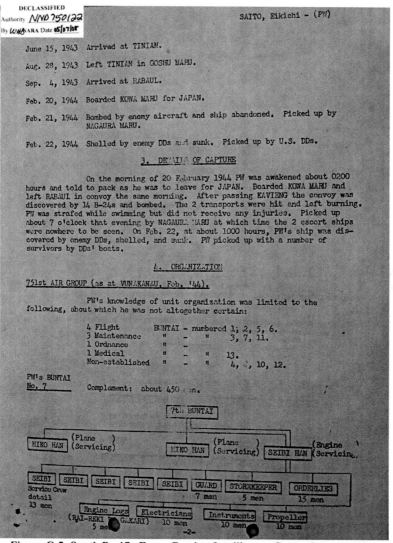

SAITO, Eikichi - (PW)

June 15, 1943   Arrived at TINIAN.

Aug. 28, 1943   Left TINIAN in GOSHU MARU.

Sep. 4, 1943   Arrived at RABAUL.

Feb. 20, 1944   Boarded KOWA MARU for JAPAN.

Feb. 21, 1944   Bombed by enemy aircraft and ship abandoned. Picked up by
                 NAGAURA MARU.

Feb. 22, 1944   Shelled by enemy DDs and sunk. Picked up by U.S. DDs.

3. DETAILS OF CAPTURE

On the morning of 20 February 1944 PW was awakened about 0200 hours and told to pack as he was to leave for JAPAN. Boarded KOWA MARU and left RABAUL in convoy the same morning. After passing KAVIENG the convoy was discovered by 14 B-24s and bombed. The 2 transports were hit and left burning. PW was strafed while swimming but did not receive any injuries. Picked up about 7 o'clock that evening by NAGAURA MARU at which time the 2 escort ships were nowhere to be seen. On Feb. 22, at about 1000 hours, PW's ship was discovered by enemy DDs, shelled, and sunk. PW picked up with a number of survivors by DDs' boats.

4. ORGANIZATION

751st AIR GROUP (as at VUNAKANAU, Feb. '44).

PW's knowledge of unit organization was limited to the following, about which he was not altogether certain:

4 Flight	BUNTAI - numbered	1, 2, 5, 6.
3 Maintenance	" - "	3, 7, 11.
1 Ordnance	" -	
1 Medical	" - "	13.
Non-established	" - "	4, 9, 10, 12.

PW's BUNTAI
No. 7   Complement: about 450 men.

7th BUNTAI

HIKO HAN (Plane) (Servicing)   HIKO HAN (Plane) (Servicing)   SEIBI HAN (Engine) (Servicing)

SEIBI SEIBI SEIBI SEIBI SEIBI   GUARD   STOREKEEPER   ORDERLIES
Service Crew
detail
13 men   7 men   5 men   15 men

(RAI-REKI GAKARI) Engine Logs   Electricians 10 men   Instruments 10 men   Propeller 10 men
5 men

-2-

**Figure C-5: South Pacific Force Combat Intelligence Center Interrogation
Report.**

SAITO, Eikichi - (PW)

Duties of HIKO HAN (Plane Servicing Sections) - PW was not familiar with details; presumed checked flying controls, struts, landing gear, etc.

5. IDENTIFICATION OF OTHER UNITS

CV RYUJO — In task force in attacks cn DAVAO and ANAMBAS I. (Jan/Feb '42). Sunk in vicinity o SOLOMONS. Date unrecalled and unable to localize closer.

OMINATO KOKUTAI — PW did not know of any other identification for this air group. It was a torpedo bomber unit using Type 97 "KATE" and Type 94 light reconnaissance twin-float biplanes (Nov. '41).

FIGHTER KOKUTAI at SABANG — PW heard that before he came to SABANG there was a fighter unit attached to the KANOYA KOKUTAI. He believed it was either the SAN KU or the ICHI KU (probably part o the 3rd or 1st Air Group). He did not know any particulars about the unit as it was gone before PW joined the unit (Oct. '42).

YON KU (4th Air Group) — This medium bomber unit (ETTY) was based at VUNAKANAU prior to the 751st. Name char ed o 702nd KOKUTAI and later, all the planes and material w re nded over to the 751st, and personnel returned to JAPAN (No . ' .).

TORPEDO BOMBER UNIT — From November 1943, an unidentified unit of torpedo bombers was based at VUNAKANAU. PW believed it came off a carrier but did not hear which. There were about 50 planes based at VUNAKANAU among them were some Type 99 dive bombers. It was possible that some of the flights were actually based at other airfields in the vicinity. No other information developed.

SETSUEI TAI — Personnel of the construction battalions at VUNAKANAU appeared to be Koreans and Formosans. Their only equipment was 3 or 4 steam rollers and a few trucks. Numbered several hundred but actual strength and unit identifications unknown.

KOWA MARU — Estimated about 1500 tons, about 12 knots. There were only 5 twin 13mm MGs on board, one each on the stern and bow, 3 on the bridge. Sunk 21 Feb. by bombs.

6. IDENTIFICATION OF PERSONALITIES

ICHIMARU, Toshinosuke	Rear Adm.	- CinC of all KOKUTAIs in the SOPAC Area.
SATA, Naohiro	Comdr.	- CO of 751st KOKUTAI.
ODA, Shichiro	Comdr.	- former CO of all SEIBI BUNTAIs in 751st.
YAJITA	Lt. Comdr.	- dical Officer of 751st.
SETOGUCHI	Lt. Comdr.	- CO of all SEIBI BUNTAIs of 751st.

-3-

Figure C-6: South Pacific Force Combat Intelligence Center Interrogation Report.

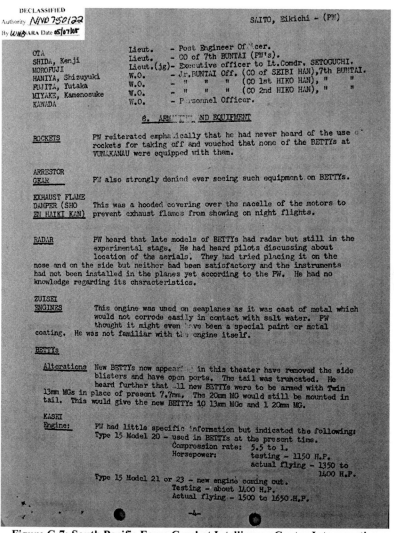

SAITO, Eikichi - (PW)

OTA   Lieut. - Post Engineer Officer.
SHIDA, Kenji   Lieut. - CO of 7th BUNTAI (PW's).
MOROFUJI   Lieut.(jg)- Executive officer to Lt.Comdr. SETOGUCHI.
HANIYA, Shizuyuki   W.O. - Jr.BUNTAI Off. (CO of SEIBI HAN),7th BUNTAI.
FUJITA, Yutaka   W.O. - " " " (CO 1st HIKO HAN), " "
MIYAKE, Kamenosuke   W.O. - " " " (CO 2nd HIKO HAN), " "
KAWADA   W.O. - Personnel Officer.

6. ARMAMENT AND EQUIPMENT

ROCKETS   PW reiterated emphatically that he had never heard of the use of rockets for taking off and vouched that none of the BETTYs at VUNAKANAU were equipped with them.

ARRESTOR GEAR   PW also strongly denied ever seeing such equipment on BETTYs.

EXHAUST FLAME DAMPER (SHO EN HAIKI KAN)   This was a hooded covering over the nacelle of the motors to prevent exhaust flames from showing on night flights.

RADAR   PW heard that late models of BETTYs had radar but still in the experimental stage. He had heard pilots discussing about location of the aerials. They had tried placing it on the nose and on the side but neither had been satisfactory and the instruments had not been installed in the planes yet according to the PW. He had no knowledge regarding its characteristics.

ZUISEI ENGINES   This engine was used on seaplanes as it was cast of metal which would not corrode easily in contact with salt water. PW thought it might even have been a special paint or metal coating. He was not familiar with the engine itself.

BETTYs

Alterations   New BETTYs now appear in this theater have removed the side blisters and have open ports. The tail was truncated. He heard further that all new BETTYs were to be armed with Twin 13mm MGs in place of present 7.7mm. The 20mm MG would still be mounted in tail. This would give the new BETTYs 10 13mm MGs and 1 20mm MG.

KASEI Engine: PW had little specific information but indicated the following:
Type 15 Model 20 - used in BETTYs at the present time.
         Compression rate: 5.5 to 1.
         Horsepower: testing - 1150 H.P.
                   actual flying - 1350 to
                              1400 H.P.
       Type 15 Model 21 or 23 - new engine coming out.
         Testing - about 1400 H.P.
         Actual flying - 1500 to 1650 H.P.

-4-

Figure C-7: South Pacific Force Combat Intelligence Center Interrogation Report.

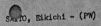
SAITO, Eikichi - (PW)

9. ENEMY METHODS

Training   Men volunteered for the YOKOSUKA Naval Maintenance Practice
Section for specialized training in airplane parts. An
examination was necessary to qualify. On enrollment, they
started in by learning the nomenclature of the different parts of the engine.
Men were then shown various engines once and then assigned to certain types.
PW was selected for KASEI engines (in particular, T-15, Model 20) which he
learned to take apart and assemble. The course was 6 months long.

12. ENEMY SUPPLIES

Engine Parts   All supplies for planes such as spare engines, small parts,
wing sections, and other miscellaneous equipment, were flown
in from JAPAN. These supplies were brought in in the replacement planes sent to the unit. When engines were damaged beyond repair,
every serviceable part was salvaged and installed as needed in emergency where
new parts were not available.

Rations   PW believed RABAUL and it. vicinity could hold out for 6 to 9
months, as that amount of supplies had been brought in and stored.

13. MORALE AND PROPAGANDA

**Service
Experience**   PW volunteered, as having an older brother in the Navy, his
ambition since a child had been to be in also. He soon found
it was not what he expected and vowed during his first year not
to make it his career. If he had a son he would do his utmost to discourage
him. He did not mind punishment when deserved but NCOs often struck without
any reason. There was no association between enlisted men and officers except
in the line of duty. Discipline was very strict aboard ship and at naval
bases, but was relaxed in combat area.

**Inter-Service
relations**   PW did not think much of army air units and had heard that
their equipment was inferior. However, there were times he
wished he was in the army because of the treatment he had
received. Army disciplined on the spot but in the navy, chastising gangs
worked on delinquents at night with a board slat and sometimes with an iron
rod. Could not say anything about cooperation between the two branches as his
duties never brought him in contact with the army.

**Others in
Forces**   PW had a brother who was an instructor at the MAIZURU Repair
Dept.   Believed he was a CPO. Another brother had been
called up three times in an army transport regiment from
FUKUSHIMA.

Mail   Since he had several brothers and sisters he received many
letters. They never commented on domestic conditions. PW
only used post cards when replying as he also could not tell
them of his environment. Mail was always censored so once, when he arrived

-5-

**Figure C-8: South Pacific Force Combat Intelligence Center Interrogation
Report.**

SAITO, Eikichi - (PW)

in YOKOSUKA, he mailed a letter in town telling his brother about his experiences and treatment and cautioned him not to enlist.

Conditions in JAPAN

PW was not familiar with conditions in JAPAN. Had heard that they were better compared to the pre-war days, as everyone - including the rich, were on an equal footing with regard to commodities.

Attitude toward capture

PW expressed the usual conventionalized views regarding disgrace and dishonor of becoming PW, and impossibility of returning to JAPAN. No ideas regarding post-war.

Allied PsW

PW had never seen any Allied PsW anywhere. He heard that there were some around RABAUL and that was all.

Morale

PW did not like VUNAKANAU. There were many things he did not like but strafing by the medium bombers and fighters was the worst experience.

Allied Leaflets

PW saw and read one leaflet dropped by an enemy plane. He thought it was very foolish as the enemy should know that it was impossible to surrender. The leaflet mentioned something about JAPAN losing many ships and having a difficult time supplying RABAUL, but he had been told by his CO that morale in JAPAN was strong and it was willing to support the army and navy until the last.

Radio

No radio available to enlisted men.

War News

Printed bulletins contained a summary of news daily. He believed it was true but it generalized and probably omitted to mention much that actually happened.

14. ENEMY INTENTIONS

KESSEN BUTAI (Decisive Battle Force)

The unit CO had told the men that they had to hold VUNAKANAU until April, as the KESSEN BUTAI was expected then from BURMA to make a final assault on AUSTRALIA. This Force was supposedly composed of army, navy, and air units and its strength larger than any army or fleet. In planes alone, it would have over 10,000. PW repeatedly stated this was one reason why the 751st and other units were not getting any replacement during the latter part of 1943 and early part of 1944. He did not know any particulars concerning the Force, except that the advance echelon was now in training in BURMA. PW sincerely believed that if this force did not reach NEW BRITAIN by early May, JAPAN would lose the war inside of a year and a half.

-6-

Figure C-9: South Pacific Force Combat Intelligence Center Interrogation Report.

CONFIDENTIAL

S..ITO, Eikichi - (PW)

Reinforcing of
rear bases — When the 751st KOKUTAI heard of the approaching enemy task force on TRUK, it sent a part of its planes to intercept or reinforce. Some of the ground personnel for maintenance of this detachment at TRUK were on the KOWA MARU with PW when it was sunk. PW thought they were to be flown back to TRUK from PALAU.

16. CHEMICAL WARFARE

PW received some training concerning the wearing of the gas masks and identification of various g...s. All personnel at VUNAKANAU were issued masks as there were rumors that U.S. would resort to gas warfare when the going got tough. He sincerely believed that JAPAN would not use poison gas though there was a possibility that she might in the case she had to make her last stand, but that was yet to come.

17. MILITARY AND NAVAL BASES

SABANG
Airfield   In Oct. '42 the field was still under construction and nearby hills were being cut away to make runways. He believed the airfield was about 1000 meters (3300') long and 100 meters (330') wide. The runway was not paved with asphalt or cement, but a surface mixture of dirt, rock and coral was used. There were no hangars or repair shops and open dispersal was used as at VUNAKANAU.

TINIAN
Airfield   This field was the best field PW had been on. The runway was about 1300 meters (4300') long and 200 meters (650') wide, asphalt-paved E-W. There was only one hangar which was used for repairing planes and engines. There were other small temporary shacks which were used as repair shops. All buildings were situated on the north side of the field. There was a small wireless tower near the headquarters building, also on the north side of the field.

VUNAKANAU
Airfield   The runways only were paved with cement. The other aprons and dispersal lanes were dirt. Volcanic dust was severe and fouled oil lines. There was no way to prevent this and it necessitated constant watching and cleaning.

18. MEDICAL

Sanitary measures were strictly enforced at VUNAKANAU and he believed this was responsible for the low incidence of malaria, dysentery and dengue fever. Each man was ordered to take 2 atabrine pills a day.

19. ENEMY INFORMATION CONCERNING ALLIES

Parafrag
Bombs   PW believed that the parafrag bombs caused most of the damage to VUNAKANAU Airfield and personnel. However, possibly one-third of the bombs dropped were duds, according to a survey made after one of the attacks.

-7-

Figure C-10: South Pacific Force Combat Intelligence Center Interrogation Report.

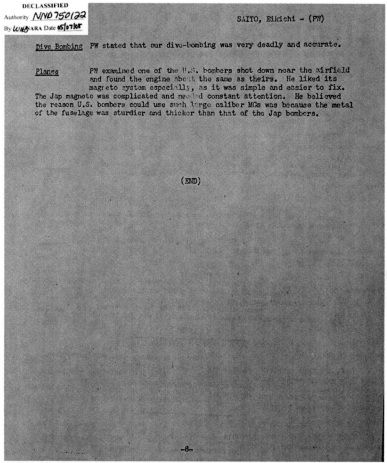

SAITO, Eikichi - (PW)

Dive Bombing   PW stated that our dive-bombing was very deadly and accurate.

Planes   PW examined one of the U.S. bombers shot down near the airfield
and found the engine about the same as theirs. He liked its
magneto system especially, as it was simple and easier to fix.
The Jap magneto was complicated and needed constant attention. He believed
the reason U.S. bombers could use such large caliber MGs was because the metal
of the fuselage was sturdier and thicker than that of the Jap bombers.

(END)

-8-

Figure C-11: South Pacific Force Combat Intelligence Center Interrogation Report.

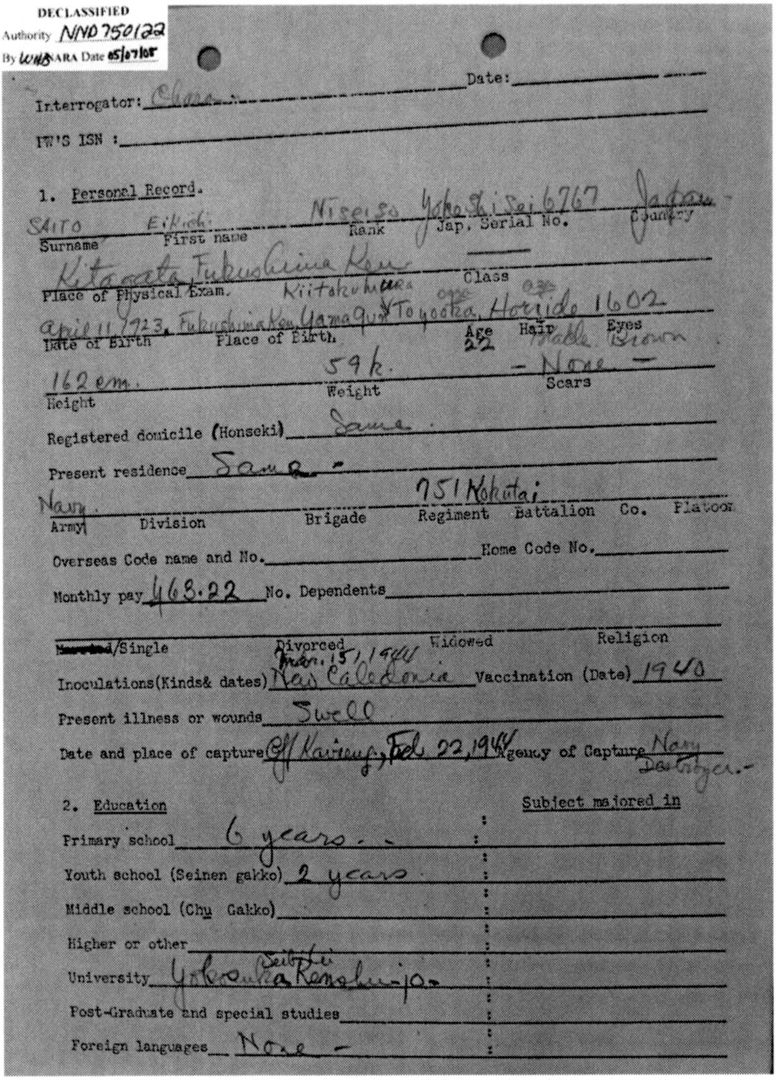

Figure C-12: Angel Island Screening Sheet.

Upon arrival at Angel Island, POWs were rescreened, based on updated collection requirements, to establish a priority list of POWs for interrogation at Camp Tracy.

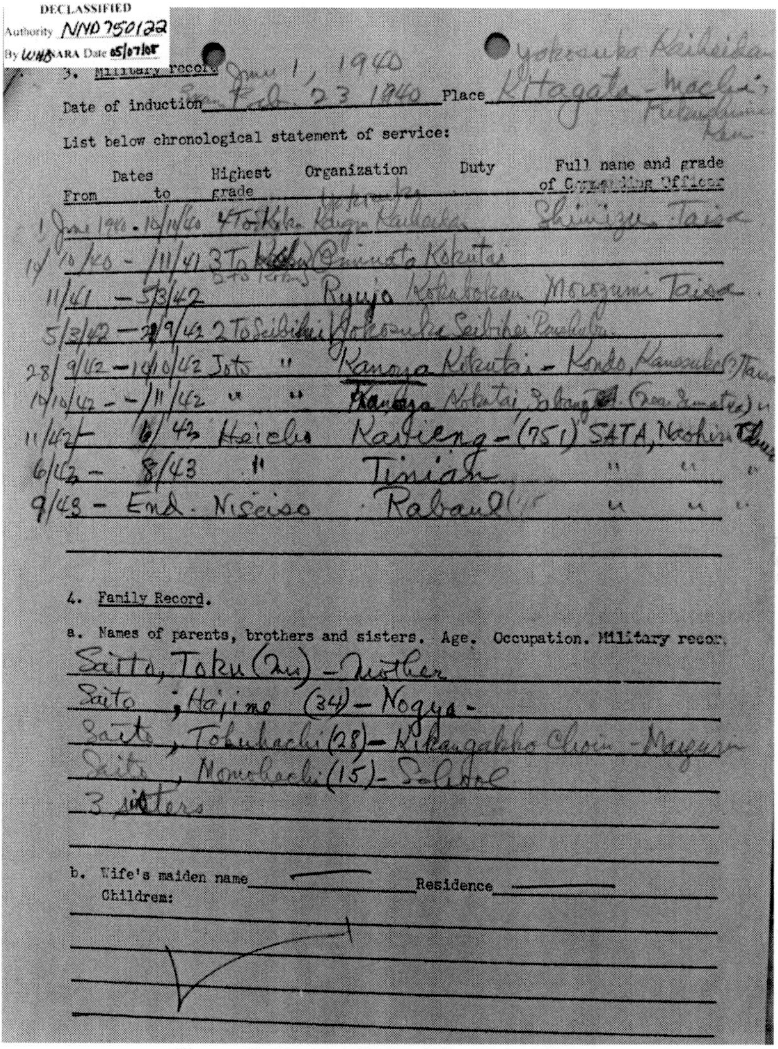

3. Military record

Date of induction _Feb. 23 1940_ Place _Kitagata-machi_

List below chronological statement of service:

Dates		Highest	Organization	Duty	Full name and grade
From	to	grade			of Commanding Officer
June 1940	10/10/40		4 Toi Koku Kangu Kaikaikai		Shimizu Taisa
10/10/40	11/41		3 To Koku @minato Kokutai		
11/41	5/3/42		Ryujo Kokubokan		Morozumi Taisa
5/3/42	28/9/42		2 To Seibitai Yokosuka Seibhei Paralyka		
28/9/42	10/10/42	Joto	"	Kanoya Kokutai - Kondo, Kanosuko Taisa	
10/10/42	11/42	"	"	Kanoya Nokotai, Sobay (near Sumatra)	
11/42	6/43		Hoichu	Kaitieng - (751) SATA, Neshin Tai	
6/43	8/43	"		Tinian	" " "
9/43	End.	Niseiso	Rabaul	" " "

4. Family Record.

a. Names of parents, brothers and sisters. Age. Occupation. Military record.

Saito, Toku (2u) - Mother

Saito ; Hajime (34) - Nogyu -

Saito, Tokuhachi (28) - Nikangakko Choin - Maguan

Saito, Momohachi (15) - School

3 sisters

b. Wife's maiden name _____ Residence _____
Children:

Figure C-13: Angel Island Screening Sheet.

c. Names and addresses of relatives and close friends residing abroad.

None.

5. Civilian occupations (Start with last position and work back to first position PW held. Outline only.)

Farm —

6. Travel *Tokyo -*

7. Hobbies - *Books —, Games, Magazines.*

8. Home Town Information *Small town — 5/600 license. Farming only. About 5 mi from Wakamatou.*

9. Attitude of PF *Extremely cooperative*

10. Estimate of personality *Bright + Pleasant*

11. Recommended approach for further interrogation *DB, Tinian, Kavieng, Commate., Rabaul, Airplane + airplane motors.*

Figure C-14: Angel Island Screening Sheet.

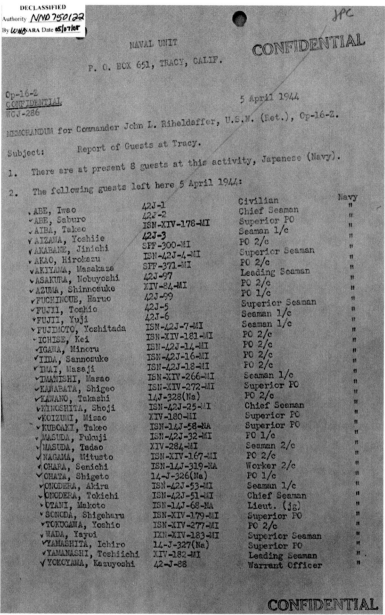

Figure C-15: Camp Tracy POW Transfer Memorandum.

To maintain accountabilty of the POWs, Camp Tracy kept meticulous records indicating the arrival and departure of POWs

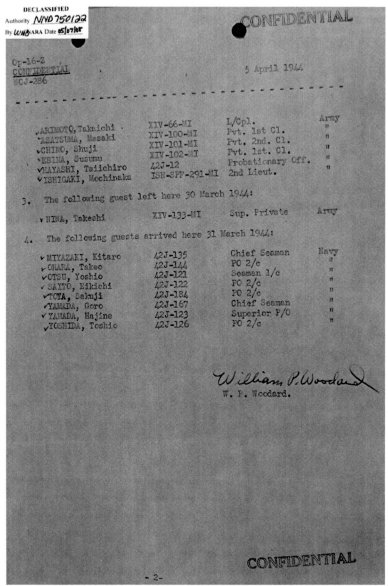

Op-16-Z
CONFIDENTIAL
WCJ-286

CONFIDENTIAL

5 April 1944

ARIMOTO, Takaichi	XIV-66-MI	L/Cpl.	Army
ASATSUMA, Masaki	XIV-100-MI	Pvt. 1st Cl.	"
CHINO, Shuji	XIV-101-MI	Pvt. 2nd. Cl.	"
EBINA, Susumu	XIV-102-MI	Pvt. 1st. Cl.	"
MAYASHI, Taiichiro	42J-12	Probationary Off.	"
ISHIGAKI, Mochinaka	ISN-SPP-291-MI	2nd Lieut.	"

3.   The following guest left here 30 March 1944:

NIWA, Takeshi	XIV-133-MI	Sup. Private	Army

4.   The following guests arrived here 31 March 1944:

MIYAZAKI, Kitaro	42J-135	Chief Seaman	Navy
OHARA, Takeo	42J-144	PO 2/c	"
OTSU, Yoshio	42J-121	Seaman 1/c	"
SAITO, Eikichi	42J-122	PO 2/c	"
TOYA, Sakuji	42J-184	PO 2/c	"
YAMADA, Goro	42J-167	Chief Seaman	"
YAMADA, Hajime	42J-123	Superior P/O	"
YOSHIDA, Toshio	42J-126	PO 2/c	"

William P. Woodard

W. P. Woodard.

CONFIDENTIAL

- 2 -

Figure C-16: Camp Tracy POW Transfer Memorandum.

from the facility. Note that the author of this memorandum, Navy LT William P. Woodard, uses the word "guests" instead of "POWs" to further obfuscate Camp Tracy's purpose.

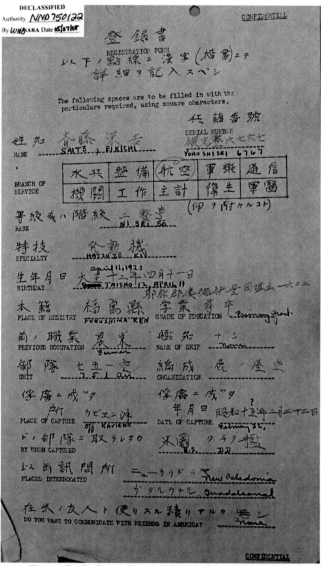

Figure C-17: Camp Tracy POW In-Processing Sheet.

Once POWs arrived at Camp Tracy they underwent a final screening, to verify the information the POW gave at earlier screenings as well as to provide data points for the interrogation plan.

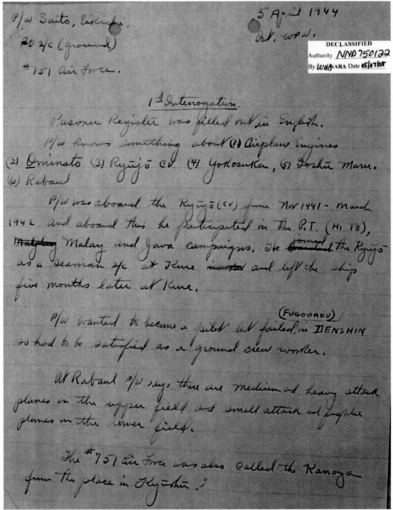

Figure C-18: Camp Tracy Interrogator Notes.

Based on their initial interviews with the POWs, interrogators would take notes to determine what files to review and what lines of questioning to pursue. This interview also served as a final check to determine whether the POW was deemed to possess strategic-level information and therefore be slated for a full interrogation.

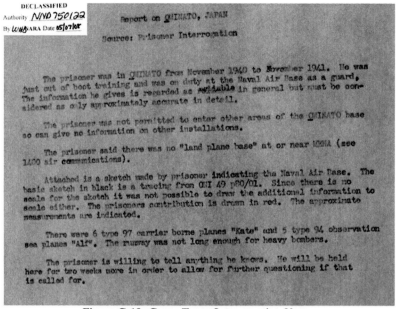

Figure C-19: Camp Tracy Interrogation Notes.

To accompany POW sketches of facilities and bases, interrogators would provide a short written report detailing the information gained from the POW. This information would then be used to update the country files for future interrogations of other POWs. The next figure shows the map that PO 2/C Saito drew of the Ominato Naval Air Base in Japan.

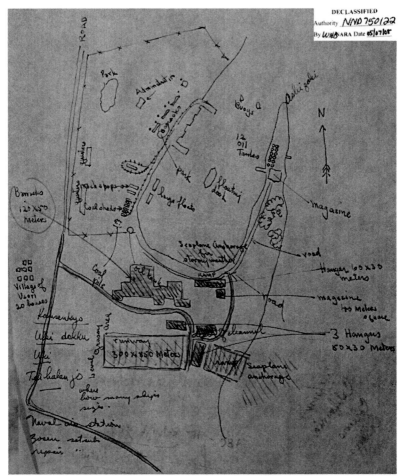

Figure C-20: Camp Tracy Interrogation Sketch.

Maps and sketches were an important product of interrogations. Because of POWs' detailed accounts, interrogators were able to provide intelligence products with vital targeting information for strategic bombing campaigns, as well as providing valuable information concerning Japanese Naval and Air Bases' capabilities.

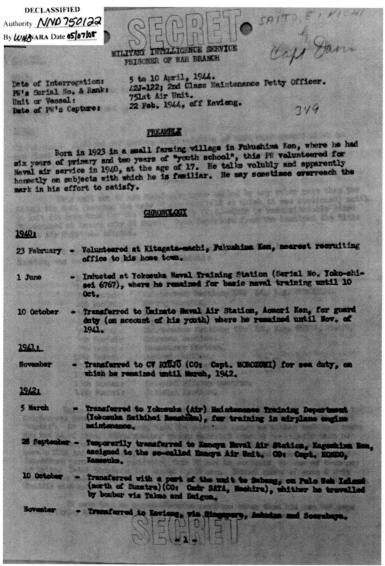

Figure C-21: Camp Tracy Interrogation Report.

The following report is the product of an interrogation at Camp Tracy that took six days to complete. Of particular strategic importance was PO 2/C Saito's knowledge of aircraft engine capabilities, weapon systems, and functional characteristics.

SECRET

5 to 10 Apr 44

1943:

June   - Transferred to Tinian.

September - Transferred to Rabaul.

1944:

22 February- Captured off Kavieng after sinking of KOWA MARU aboard which he and about half of his unit were headed for Tenian via Palau.
a quarter

UNIT

PW's unit was to his knowledge never called by any other name than the KANOYA Air Unit (bearing the name of the airfield at which it was stationed) until it left its home base for the South Pacific (I.N.—This is understandable since PW remained at Kanoya only 10 days). Upon departure from the homeland the title "751st Air Unit" was adopted.

PW asserts that this medium bomber unit, commanded by Cmdr. SATA, Naohiro, was composed of 14 Sections (Buntai):

1st Buntai:	Flying Section (Buntai).
2nd Buntai:	Flying Section.
3rd Buntai:	Maintenance Section; CO: Lt. j.g. MOROTUJI.
4th Buntai:	Flying Section.
5th Buntai:	Flying Section.
6th Buntai:	Flying Section.
7th Buntai:	Maintenance Section; CO: Lt. j.g. SHIDA, Kenji.
8th Buntai:	Ordnance Section.
9th Buntai:	Intendance Section.
10th Buntai:	Medical Section.
11th Buntai:	Maintenance Section.
12th Buntai:	Repair Section.
13th Buntai:	Internal Affairs Section.
14th Buntai:	Judicial Section.

While PW asserts that he is certain of the numbering of the Flying and Maintenance Sections, he is doubtful of the numbers of the other miscellaneous "buntai". He insists, however, that the sections exist as stated and that there are but 14 of them. Since another PW has asserted equally positively that he himself belonged to an 18th Buntai, which was the Medical Section, and that there were a 17th and a 19th Buntai, which were Truck Drivers and Electricians, and Intendance personnel, respectively, this PW may be confused, or one of them may be lying. Total personnel was around 2,000 men. Formal quota of such a unit should have been 75 planes, but the unit actually started operations in the South Pacific with only 50.

PW says that he cannot describe sections other than his own but says that a Flying Section was made up of about 100 men including:

SECRET

- 2 -

Figure C-22: Camp Tracy Interrogation Report.

SECRET

5 to 10 Apr 44

Pilots   Observers
Bombardiers   Radiomen
           Gunners

A maintenance section (of which there were 3), was divided into 3 groups (or Bu).

   1st Bu (Hikōbu) —Plane maintenance personnel, who attended upkeep and
        minor repairs other than to the plane engines—about 150 men.
   2nd Bu (Hikōbu) —Plane maintenance personnel—about 150 men.
   3rd Bu (Sei Bu) —Engine maintenance personnel—about 100 men.

The 3rd Bu was composed of 15/16 Carburetor specialists, 15/16 Electric Gauge specialists, 15/16 Mechanical Gauge specialists and about 50 general engine repairers.

The 3rd Buntai was responsible for the maintenance and repairs of the engines of planes used by the 1st and 2nd Buntai. The 7th and 11th Buntai were responsible for planes of the 5th and 6th Bu and the 4th Bu respectively.

The 12th Buntai attended major repairs which could not be attended by the regular maintenance personnel in the 3rd, 7th and 11th Buntai.

When PW left Kavoya, he was a member of a small detachment sent on special duty to Sabang. The unit took off in about six bombers, and flew to Sabang via Takao (Formosa) and Saigon (FIC)—both single night stands. This detachment remained at Sabang for only one month, until ordered to rejoin the main strength of the unit at Kavieng, travelling by an unidentified, small freighter via Singapore, Soerabaya and Amboina (1 or 2 days in each port).

The unit remained at Kavieng until June, 1943, when it was again transferred in unidentified freighters to Rabaul, where three quarters of it (about 1,500 men) probably remains to this day, the remainder having been ordered out "to increase the strength of the Mandates". The detail to the Mandates, of which PW was a member, was sunk off Kavieng, aboard the KONA MARU.

OTHER UNITS

702ND AIR UNIT: This was a medium bomber unit similar in organization to the 751st. It preceded the 751st in the Mountain (Yamano) Airfield near Rabaul, leaving there immediately upon the arrival of the 751st to take over, and leaving some of its planes and material to its successor.

PW heard that this unit had been known as the 4th Air Unit prior to October, 1942, when a radical change was made in the designation of all air units, presumably in the interests of secrecy.

MEDIUM BOMBER UNITS:

        Taikyu Air Unit.
        Takao Air Unit.

SECRET

- 3 -

Figure C-23: Camp Tracy Interrogation Report.

SECRET   5 to 10 Apr 44

Genzan Air Unit.
Mihoro Air Unit.
Misawa Air Unit.

PW had heard of the first four units while in training at Yokosuka in 1942. The Genzan and Mihoro Units gained fame with the Kanoya Unit in the sea-battle off Malaya. He heard later of the Misawa Unit as another Medium Bomber Unit. The first four units bear the names of their home airbases. He had never heard of the Genzan or Misawa Units being based at Rabaul (I.N.—As mentioned by another PW).

253RD AIR UNIT (NAVAL): PW believes that the 253rd Air Unit, a fighter unit based at one of the other fields near Rabaul, provided fighter escort for the 751's bombers when they went on a mission.

NUMBERING OF UNITS: PW believes that the fixed pattern for the number-ing of various types of naval air units runs as follows (I.N.—Queries are placed after items of which PW seemed very uncertain):

SERIES:	TYPE OF UNIT:
0-99	Fighter (?).
100-199	Fighter (?).
200-299	Fighter.
300-399	Carrier-based assault (Kanjo Kogeki).
400-499	Hydroplane (sui-jō hikōtai).
500-599	Some type of hydroplane (?).
600-699	Large type hydroplane (Ōgata suitei).
700-799	?
800-899	?
900-999	Transport.

(I.N.—Supporting evidence for this pattern is found in the fact that the 251st and 253rd Air Units are known to be fighter groups, while the 753rd, PW's own outfit, and 702nd, which PW has mentioned in connection with Rabaul, were both bomber units. Unfortunately PW can give no specific examples of other types of units.)

MITSUBISHI TYPE 1 MEDIUM BOMBER (BETTY)

Crew: 2 Pilots   1 Bombardier
          2 Radiomen   1 Tail Gunner
          1 Engineer

Armament: One 7.7 mm MG in nose turret.
           Two 7.7 mm MG in each lateral blister.
           One 20 mm MG in tail turret.

PW believes that the 5 single-barrelled MG's are to be replaced by twin-barrelled 13 mm cannon, to increase firepower.

SECRET

- 4 -

Figure C-24: Camp Tracy Interrogation Report.

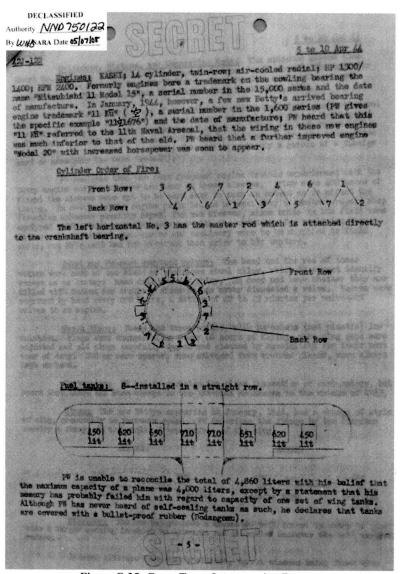

Figure C-25: Camp Tracy Interrogation Report.

5 to 10 Apr 44

Cylinders, Pistons, and Connecting Rods: The attached sketch (See Chart No. 106) has been adapted from rough sketches by PW showing the cylinder head and piston now used in Betty Bombers. PW says that a slightly concave piston head replaced the former flat-topped head in October, 1943.

The sleeves or liners of the holes at either end of the connecting rod (fitting around the crankshaft and boss on the piston), the damper bearing and the main bearing are made of Kerumetto (ケルメット)(I.N.--A soft brass-like yellow metal, probably similar to babbit-metal. PW cannot give the composition of or otherwise describe this metal; the name is probably a garble of a foreign word or name plus the word "metal").

PW declares that the most frequent engine trouble experienced with the Betty engine was due to wear and tear on these sleeves. After some 400 hours of flight the sleeves were apt to be worn away to such an extent as to affect the timing. In such case the engine parts had to be sent away to another repair shop (location unknown; possibly Japan) for new sleeves, since units in the field were equipped neither with spare sleeves nor with the machinery for replacing them. It was understood that such spares and machinery were to be supplied to field units, but PW's unit had not received them prior to his capture.

Inlet and Exhaust Overhead valves: The head and the rod of these valves were made of two kinds of stainless steel alloy, which PW cannot identify except as to luster: head dull and rod shiny. He does not know whether they are filled with sodium for cooling, since he has never dissected a valve. Valves were reground by hand every 400 hours, a matter of 40 to 45 minutes per valve--28 valves to an engine.

Spark Plugs: These had three points, with porcelain (not plastic) insulation. Plugs were changed after every 60 hours of flying, when plug gaps were adjusted and old plugs carefully tested and cleaned by specialists for their next tour of duty. 200 or more spares, some salvaged from wrecked planes, were always kept on hand.

Carburetor: PW had no occasion for close inspection of carburetors, but heard that there was some change in the internal mechanism in the autumn of 1943.

Wings: The new Bettys appearing in January, 1944, had a change of style of wing, presumably to increase speed. PW describes the change by two diagrams showing a change in the angle of top surface of the wing.

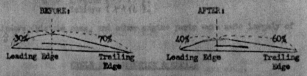

BEFORE:	AFTER:
30% 70%	40% 60%
Leading Edge Trailing Edge	Leading Edge Trailing Edge

Fuselage: The new Bettys have a truncated tail turret in order to provide a larger opening in which to traverse and otherwise maneuver the tail machine cannon.

Lateral blisters have been abolished, turret windows being flush with

- 6 -

Figure C-26: Camp Tracy Interrogation Report.

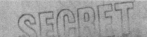

5 to 10 Aug 44

the sides of the body.

Landing Gear: The tail wheel of the new Betty is retractible, while that of its predecessor is not.

Oil: No. 1 Heavy Airplane Oil, changed every 30 hours. Capacity of tanks was 150 liters, but normal load was 130 liters.

Armor: The Betty has no armor. Windshield and turret glass, however, are of non-shatterable glass (anzen-garasu), penetrable only by AA shells, as is the glass door between the tail turret and the toilet-room. PW heard that there was soon to be an increase in wing armor.

In Rabaul PW saw three-piece suits of armor for flying personnel, consisting of two greaves and a breast-plate tailored to fit the body, but to his knowledge these were never used.

Oxygen Tanks: Two large tubes of oxygen were installed in the fuselage, one on either side, from which copper tubes with outlets for attachment of the rubber tubes of the masks extended along the walls. The flying engineer was in charge of the oxygen apparatus.

Tires: Tires bore the trademark "Daidō Tire" (大日タイヤ).

Fire Extinguishers: Planes were equipped with carbonic-acid-gas extinguishers, 2 hand-operated in the nacelle of each engine and 5 automatic (set in operation by heat) in the fuselage. These extinguishers were about 2 feet long and 6 inches in diameter.

Instruments: Instruments were manufactured by the Nakajima Airplane works and bore the trade-mark "Nakajima" (中島) with a number starting with 15, almost certainly of 5 digits.

Materials: Wings and fuselage were constructed largely of DURALUMINUM, which PW describes as "SDCH":

S - Kyō (起).
D - Duraluminum.
C - Kuratto (クラツト).
H - Yakiire (ヤキイレ).

Cylinders, pistons, cams, and other engine parts were made largely of "Y Alloy" (Y合金).

CYCLE OF INSPECTION & REPAIR

Small Inspection (ShōRensa): This quick inspection, involving a checking of the timing, cylinder heads, pistons, wiring, magneto and an adjustment of valve gaps, was made after every mission—and again before the following mission if several days elapsed between flights. It took four men about an hour to complete the job on a plane; in an emergency as many as 7 men would be assigned.

- 7 -

Figure C-27: Camp Tracy Interrogation Report.

5 to 10 Apr 44

423-122

Medium Inspection (Chūkensa): This inspection, involving overhauling of cylinders, pistons, connecting rods and cam shaft, was made every 300 hours, taking four or five men 5 or 6 days to complete.

Large Inspection (Daikensa): This inspection, involving a complete breakdown of the motor, grinding of valves, and cleaning and oiling of parts usually took about 10 days. Four or five men did the stripping and 15 to 16 men did the cleaning, oiling and repairs. It was almost invariably necessary to have the "Kerumetto" bearing sleeves replaced at every "large inspection." The grinding of valves was always the final job because of the time involved. Valves were never replaced with spares unless absolutely necessary, since this involved a very careful adjustment of gaps. Few planes survived the 400 hours for a "large inspection" at Rabaul.

Spare Parts: The maintenance Buntai usually maintained a supply of from 3 to 6 spares for all engine parts, many salvaged from wrecked or damaged planes.

Welding and other heavy repairs: Effected by the "Repair Buntai".

Fueling: PW believes that a tank truck, capacity either 3,200 or 4,200 liters, could fill a 600 liter tank in about 5 minutes. There were three trucks to each maintenance Buntai.

CIVILIAN SPECIALIST DEPOTS (KŌKUSHO)

All repairs are usually made by the Repair Buntai of the Air Unit, but at some airbases there are civilian specialist depots attached to the unit, in which case all complicated repair jobs are handed over to them. There were such depots at Vunakanau and Tenian. Except for the replacing of the "Kerumetto" sleeves, practically no repair jobs are sent away for attention elsewhere. Minor repairs are attended first, while big jobs are left for attention during spare time.

PW does not know the status of these depots but believes that they are operated by private aircraft companies, perhaps Mitsubishi, when planes of the unit are Bettys. The specialists, mostly ex-military men without uniform, receive very attractive wages. They possess better tools than those of the Maintenance and Repair Buntai of the Air Units.

BOMBS AND TORPEDOES

The normal load of a bomber was:

Four No. 6 Rikuyō (land) Bombs (60 kilograms each)
and Two No. 25 Bombs (250 kilograms each)
or
Twelve No. 6 Rikuyō Bombs
or
One Marine Torpedo (800 kilograms).

- 8 -

Figure C-28: Camp Tracy Interrogation Report.

SECRET

5 to 10 Apr 44

Bombs and torpedoes were loaded by the Ordnance Buntai, which lifted the ammunition into position by means of heavy portable jacks, which PW had heard of but had not seen.

LOCATIONS

ALUMINUM PLANT, KITAGATA MACHI (喜多方町), FUKUSHIMA KEN: Just prior to his enlistment (1941) PW saw an area on the southern outskirts of the small town of Kitagata being cleared for building. It was rumored to be the site of a new aluminum plant. In 1942 he received letters from home saying that the plant had been completed and had drawn a large influx of workers.

The only large factory in the town theretofore was the installation of the Maruzen (or Maruyama) Silk Reeling Co. Ltd., a group of 5 or 6 wood and concrete buildings with tile roofs, employing perhaps 2,000 men and women.

KANOYA AIRFIELD, KAGOSHIMA KEN (SEPT. 1942): PW believes that this airfield is the largest in Japan. It had a very large landing field without runways, covered with short grass, 3 immense steel-framed corrugated iron hangars with concrete floors, many two-storied concrete barracks and a large repair shop. PW cannot describe the field in detail since he was there only a few days.

SABANG AIRFIELD, PULO WEH ISLAND (North of Sumatra - Oct/Nov. 1942): This was a new field still under construction. It was situated between Lake BERGMEER and the east coast of the island, about 1/2 hour by truck southeast of the town of Sabang. The single runway, 1,000 meters by 4/500 meters, was paved with crushed coral. The surrounding field in which PW's detachment from the 751st Air Unit kept its six planes was covered with knee-deep grass and had no hangars or revetments. Water supply was brought from Lake Bergmeer. Lights in the barracks were powered by spare airplane batteries, one big battery in each barracks, lighting three small airplane bulbs. The bulbs were shaded with a cloth, for blackout regulations were very severe. Men often went to bed as early as 6 p.m. The batteries lasted only about three days, after which they were re-charged by a small gasoline-driven dynamo. Recharging took about four hours.

PW declares himself unfamiliar with the town of Sabang, since he left the vicinity of the airfield only three times, and was permitted to visit only the main street of the town some distance from the waterfront (I.N.—That he showed very genuine surprise concerning the existence of Kelas Island, a pretty obvious landmark in the Bay, seems to corroborate this statement).

(I.N.—The attached sketch, No. 403, adapted with PW's cooperation as a projection of "Chart C.B. 1819 A 18 Dec 1937" opposite page 90 of "ONI-70, Field Monograph of Netherlands East Indies" is drawn without scale and without know-ledge of the contour of the coastline; its value lies in showing the location and the description of the airfield.)

KAVIENG AIRFIELD, NEW IRELAND (JUNE, 1943): (I.N.—See attached Chart No. 401—adapted from PW's drawing and later coordinated with PW's assistance

- 9 -

SECRET

Figure C-29: Camp Tracy Interrogation Report.

/21-122

with Air Photo on Page 9 of December, 1943, issue of "Impact"). Headquarters, a white wooden building on a slope overlooking the sea was easily distinguishable from the other more somber buildings.

Guns shown in chart were two-barrelled pieces of about 5 inches in caliber (model unknown). Searchlights, shown in the chart with queries, were never actually seen by the PW, who saw only their beams originating from the localities marked (south of the airfield).

Although PW cannot locate fuel or ammunition dumps, he saw gasoline drums stacked amid the palms south of the field. He heard that running water was pumped by motor from a spring south of the field. Rainwater also was caught to replenish the supply. Men were supposed to boil water for drinking but frequently drank directly from the faucets.

TINIAN ISLAND, MARIANA ARCHIPELAGO (Sept. 1943): PW's unit left Kavieng with the expectation of returning to Japan; hence, when the men were put ashore in Tinian Harbor, there was general disappointment. Landing was by small motorboats operated by Japanese civilians who, PW thought, were fishermen or employees of the sugar company in the town. The transport left immediately that night, for it was reported that Tinian Harbor was a popular hunting ground for enemy submarines.

PW thought that the unit was brought to Tinian to rest, as there was not very much work to do; mechanics kept themselves busy experimenting with engines. Pilots practiced take-offs and landings.

Shown a map of Tinian, PW was surprised at the improvements. He thinks that many new buildings have been constructed since he left. Before seeing the map, he made the following comments:

Two wireless towers and an observation tower stood near the Headquarters. There were about seven wooden barracks, bigger and better than those at Kavieng, lighted by electricity (source unknown). There was running water so salty that soap would not lather. He remembers no air-raid shelters.

The one asphalt runway was about 1,500 meters in length and 350 meters in width, having one small round hangar of corrugated iron, used only as a repair shop. There were no revetments, some 200 Bettys being parked in the open around the runway.

PW is fairly certain that there was a fuel dump tunnelled into the hills about 600 meters north of the airfield, an area strictly guarded and closed to unauthorized trespassers, because he saw trucks bring fuel thence and because he heard that fuel was quickly obtainable on account of the excellent facilities in the tunnels. Some 200 drums of oil, presumably surplus which could not be accommodated within the underground dump, were stacked in an unrestricted area between field and tunnels, some 200 meters from the field and about 400 meters from the tunnelled area.

- 10 -

Figure C-30: Camp Tracy Interrogation Report.

5 to 10 Apr 44

~~.~~-122

VUNAKUNAU AIRFIELD, near Rabaul, New Ireland (Feb 1944): The Headquarters area is covered by a dense growth of trees, which probably obscures the buildings from the air. The coconut trees in the barracks area, however, probably do not provide sufficient cover to hide the buildings. PW insists that the area just south of the runway is a grassy slope containing a number of unfilled bomb craters (I.N.--Thereby disagreeing with PW 42J-88, who states that this was a level dirt stretch often used for landing). There were revetments for planes at either end of the field. PW had never visited those at the north end but believes there were more than 70 at the south end. Revetments were staggered on either side of the dispersal alleys.

The barracks and most of the buildings in the barracks area were of wood, as was the civilian repair shop. Other shops were in tents. The motor pool, housing some 15 trucks and passenger cars, consisted of various types of shelters: tents, wooden lean-to's, etc. A few of the buildings were camouflaged with paint but the majority were covered with coconut fronds for concealment.

Presumably the fuel dump was in the hills to the northeast, as trucks carrying gasoline drums came thence. Oil drums, less inflammable than gasoline barrels, were stored alongside the airfield at the entrance to air-raid shelters in the bomber revetments. Gasoline trucks were parked either in the motor-pool shelters or in the open alongside the barracks.

Since there was no running water at Vunakunau as at Kavieng, water was trucked from a distance in cans and distributed at various points throughout the camp for cooking, bathing and drinking. Rainwater was collected to supplement the supply.

Electric power probably came from Rabaul. Bulbs were kept covered with black cloth, since anti-airraid regulations were strict. "Lights out" was at 9 o'clock. During air-raids, all lights were extinguished by a master switch.

Each barracks was equipped with one air-raid shelter capable of sheltering about 150 men. These shelters were underground, reinforced by palm trunks, some having but one layer, others having as many as five layers. To PW's belief, enemy planes never bothered to attack this area, concentrating their bombs on the runway. Although there were shelters dug into the sides of the plane revetments, these were seldom used, as men generally returned to their own barracks' shelters during raids. Prior to PW's arrival, one of these revetment shelters had been bashed in by a bomb causing 7 casualties.

During November, 1943, formations of 20 to 60 U. S. bombers used to come over almost daily, generally between 8 and 10 in the morning or in the evening. As these times drew nigh, personnel would become restless in anticipation. An hour after the morning raid, when the "all-clear" sounded men would resume duty. The labor battalion of some 200 men (Koreans, Japanese and men from the OKINAWA Islands) would set to work on the runway in order that the field might be serviceable for night operation.

Although PW had heard of a radar station somewhere in the hills he does not know how the first warning of air attack was received. At night the warning was disseminated by means of telephones, sirens in the hills and flashes of red light from the observation towers. During the day, warnings were disseminated by means of telephones, sirens and red flags hung from the observation towers. These signals were generally given 10 or 15 minutes before the attack.

-- 11 --

Figure C-31: Camp Tracy Interrogation Report.

(See attached Sketch No. 405)

SECRET

5 to 10 Apr 44

COMMUNICATIONS

Japanese planes approaching the field at night identified themselves as friendly by means of a light blinker, according to a dot-dash code changed daily. During the day, signals were by flags and wing maneuvers.

OPERATIONAL METHODS

Formations: The unit's bombers flew groups of 3 planes, one, two, three or four groups being assigned as a squadron for a mission, depending upon the size and type of target.

Assignment of Crews: The men of the Flying Buntai were appointed to fixed crews, to which in turn specific planes were assigned, each crew always flying the same plane.

GENERAL

Individual armament of ground crews: Each man had been issued either a Model 99 (7.7 mm) or a Model 38 (6.5 mm) rifle on leaving Japan, but these had been packed in cases and carried from location to location without distribution. These rifles were left behind when the group left Rabaul.

Sinking of the CV ENIU: PW heard that the ship, on which he trained in 1941, had been sunk but knows no details of the disaster.

Anti-aircraft Hits: PW saw 1 plane downed over Vunakanau, the third plane on the left wing of a formation. It was common gossip among the troops that AA guns were never able to hit the leading plane, that strikes were always to the rear of a formation.

Recognition of Enemy Planes:

    Lockheed - by twin bodies.
    North American - by strafing tactics.
    Boeing - by slim body and slow approach.
    Consolidated - By hull and slow approach.

Dummy Planes: PW claims that dummy planes have never been used at any of the airfields at which he has been stationed.

"Evacuation" of New Britain: PW will not admit that the Japanese had any intention of ever evacuating Rabaul. From January, 1944, some dissatisfaction was apparent among the troops because only officers had cigarettes and beer, because very few transports were able to evade the submarine blockade and make port; it was rumored that ship after ship had gone down, until it was impossible to bring in supplies other than by submarine, plus a little by plane. It was generally believed, however, that the troops had an ample supply of staple commodities for a six-month stand, and that the situation would improve in the meantime. Nevertheless,

SECRET

- 12 -

Figure C-32: Camp Tracy Interrogation Report.

5 to 10 Apr 44

127-122

PW admits that the Japanese, Korean and Okinawan prostitutes were withdrawn in January and that his own group left very precipitously, orders to move having been issued at 2 a.m. and the unit being under way at 7 the same morning (20 February), ostensibly to increase the strength at Tinian or Palau against a prospective American task force. PW believes that there were no troops of other units aboard the "KUMA MARU" (2,000 tons), on which he first went down with about 200 men of the 751st under command of Lt. (sg) MOROFUJI, Shigeharu (CO of 3rd Buntai), or aboard the NAGAURA MARU (500 tons) by which he was rescued and on which he had his second ducking the following day (22 February). He cannot say whether there were other troops aboard the third transport of the convoy, the KUKAI MARU (about 3,000 tons), or the two sub-chasers (about 2,000 tons each) which escorted the convoy—all three of which may have escaped (Two destroyers were supposed to provide additional protection after the convoy put to sea, but these never appeared).

MORALE

PW gives a graphic example of the morale of Japanese troops; when the NAGAURA MARU was torpedoed, the men aboard gave three "Bansais" for the Emperor and struck up the "Kimigayo", continuing to sing until the ship submerged.

PW admits, however, that he himself believes the Japanese attitude toward prisoners of war, which forbids them ever to return to Japan, to be a barbaric tradition incompatible with modern culture.

(I.N.—For previous interrogation see CIC South Pacific Force POW Int. Report A-218).

END

- 13 -

Figure C-33: Camp Tracy Interrogation Report.

End Notes

Foreward

[1] Petula Dvorak, "Fort Hunt's Quiet Men Break Silence on WWII: Interrogator Fought 'Battle of Wits'," *The Washington Post*, October 6, 2007, http://www.washingtonpost.com/wp-dyn/content/article/2007/10/05/AR2007100502492.html (accessed November 4, 2008).

[2] Chuck Hagee, "Talk Was Their Weapon—Silence Their Legacy: Their Recognition Waved in the Morning Sun at Exactly 11:42," *Arlington Connection*, October 9, 2008, http://www.connectionnewspapers.com/article.asp?article=309498&paper=60&cat=104 (accessed November 4, 2008).

[3] Dvorak.

[4] President George W. Bush, "President Discusses Creation of Military Commissions to Try Suspected Terrorists," *Office of the Press Secretary*, Washington, DC, September 6, 2006, emphasis added, http://www.whitehouse.gov/ news/releases/2006/09/print/20060906-3.html (accessed November 4, 2008).

[5] E-mail, Steve Kleinman to Alexander D. Corbin, Subject: Re: Thesis Chapter 4, June 3, 2008, 2:02 PM.

Chapter One

[1] Office of the Director of National Intelligence, *The National Intelligence Strategy of the United States of America* (Washington, D.C.: 2005), 5, http://www.dni.gov/publications/NISOctober2005.pdf (accessed November 14, 2007).

[2] Senator Bond of Missouri, speaking for the Intelligence Authorization Act, on April 12, 2007, to the U.S. Senate, 110th Congress, 1st session, *Congressional Record*, S4407.

[3] Sheryl Gay Stolberg, "Bush Says Interrogation Methods Aren't Torture," *New York Times*, October 6, 2007, http://www.nytimes.com/ 2007/10/06/U.S./nationalspecial3/06interrogate.html (accessed November 25, 2007).

[4] See Ben Wedeman, "Shock, Outrage Over Prison Photos," *CNN.com*, May 1, 2004, http://edition.cnn.com/2004/WORLD/meast/04/30/ Iraq.photos/index.html (accessed November 30, 2007); and Richard A. Serrano, "Pentagon: Koran Defiled," *Los Angeles Times*, June 4, 2005.

[5] John W. Dower, *Embracing Defeat: Japan in the Wake of World War II* (New York: W. W. Norton & Company, 1999), 213.

[6] Thomas C. Van Cleve, *Report on the Activities of Two Agencies of the CPM Branch, MIS, G-2, WDGS, The Interrogation Section Fort Hunt, Virginia, Tracy, California and the MIS-X Section Fort Hunt Virginia,* 1946, Record Group 165, Records of the War Department General and Special Staffs; Office of the Director of Intelligence (G-2), Subordinate Office and Branches, Captured Personnel and Material Branch, National Archives and Records Administration, College Park, MD, 88.

Chapter Two

[1] At the time LTG Kimmons was the U.S. Army Deputy Chief of Staff for Intelligence, otherwise known as the U.S. Army G2, the highest U.S. Army intelligence position. See U.S. Department of Defense, "DoD News Briefing with Deputy Assistant Secretary Stimson and Lt. Gen. Kimmons from the Pentagon," *Office of the Assistant Secretary of Defense (Public Affairs)*, September 6, 2006, http://www.defenselink.mil/transcripts/ transcript.aspx?transcriptid=3712 (accessed February 11, 2008).

[2] In modern military doctrine "Joint Interrogation Centers" are now referred to as: "Joint Interrogation and Debriefing Centers" (JIDC). For

purposes of consistency and clarity, the author will continue to use the WWII term "JIC" when discussing current JIDCs.

[3] At the same time, the official U.S. Army interrogation course, called the Human Intelligence Collector Course, at Fort Huachuca, Arizona, lasted 16 weeks and 4 days. See Army Training Requirements and Resources System (ATRRS), "Human Intelligence Collector," *United States Army ATRRS*, https://atrrs.army.mil/atrrscc/courseInfo.aspx ?fy=2003&sch=301*crs=241-97E10&crstitle=HUMAN +INTELLIGENCE+COLLECTOR&phase= (accessed 11 February, 2008).

[4] Tara McKelvey, *Monstering: Inside America's Policy of Secret Interrogations and Torture in the Terror War* (New York: Carroll & Graf Publishers, 2007), 15.

[5] Reportedly the Saddam regime executed some four thousand prisoners in 1984, 123 in 2000, and twenty-three in 2001; see McKelvey, 61.

[6] As per author's personal experiences while stationed at FOB Abu Ghraib, Iraq from January to June 2004 in support of Operation Iraqi Freedom as a Military Intelligence Company Commander.

[7] McKelvey, 61. Dachau was the very first Nazi concentration camp established within Germany in 1933. It was located in the state of Bavaria, approximately ten miles northwest of Munich in southern Germany. It is estimated that nearly 25,000 "political" prisoners died at Dachau from disease and malnutrition. For more information on Dachau please see the Jewish Virtual Library at http://www.jewishvirtuallibrary.org/jsource/ Holocaust/dachau.html (accessed June 5, 2008).

[8] Steven Strasser, ed., *The Abu Ghraib Investigations: The Official Reports of the Independent Panel and the Pentagon on the Shocking Prisoner Abuse in Iraq* (New York: PublicAffairs, 2004), 11.

[9] Ibid., 63.

[10] Ibid., 11.

[11] As per author's personal experiences while stationed at FOB Abu Ghraib, Iraq from January to June 2004 in support of Operation Iraqi Freedom as a Military Intelligence Company Commander. Also see: BBC, "Iraq Jail Attack Kills 22 Inmates," *BBC News*, April 20, 2004, http://news.bbc.co.uk/2/hi/ middle_east/3643151.stm (accessed February 11, 2008).

[12] Strasser, 24.

[13] Ibid., 73.

[14] Erik Saar and Viveca Novak, *Inside the Wire: A Military Intelligence Soldier's Eyewitness Account of Life at Guantanamo* (New York: The Penguin Press, 2005), 124.

[15] Ibid., 80-81.

[16] Ibid., 182.

[17] Ibid., 191.

[18] Ibid., 192.

[19] Bob Moore and Kent Fedorowich, *The British Empire and its Italian Prisoners of War, 1940-1947* (New York: Palgrave, 2002), 10.

[20] "How War Prisoners Behave," *Science Digest*, April 1944, 30.

[21] Gorman J. Ferris, Captain, U.S. Army, "Japanese Prisoners of War," January 7, 1946; Record Group 389, Provost Marshal General, Executive Division, Technical Information Officer Publicity File, 1942-1945, NARA, College Park, MD, 2.

[22] In the realm of statecraft, "turning" an agent involves convincing a captured agent to betray his country. As the agent is converted or "turned" to another country's cause, without the original country's knowledge, the "double-agent" can then supply false information back to the original country. One of the most successful and well-known results of Camp 020's efforts was the Double Cross System that in turn played a crucial role in the deception plans surrounding the Allied invasion of Normandy. For more details see J.C. Masterman, *The Double Cross System* (New Haven: Yale University Press, 1972).

[23] Oliver Hoare, ed., *Camp 020: MI5 and the Nazi Spies* (Bath: Bath Press Ltd., 2000), 17.

[24] James A. Stone, "Interrogations of Japanese POWs in WWII: U.S. Response to a Formidable Challenge" (master's thesis, National Defense Intelligence College, 2007), 22-23.

[25] John W. Dower, *War Without Mercy: Race & Power in the Pacific War* (New York: Pantheon Books, 1986), 144.

[26] Warren J. Clear, "Close Up of the Jap Fighting Man," *Reader's Digest*, November 1942, 125.

[27] Ibid.

[28] Sidney C. Moody, Jr., *War Against Japan* (Novato: Presidio Press, 1994), 25.

[29] Ruth Benedict, *The Chrysanthemum and the Sword: Patterns of Japanese Culture* (Rutland: Charles E. Tuttle Company, 1954), 128.

[30] Moody, 78.

[31] "Translation of Sept. 11 Hijacker Mohamed Atta's Suicide Note: Part Two," *ABC News*, September 28, 2001, http://abcnews.go.com/International/Story?id=79167&page=2 (accessed February 24, 2008).

[32] National Commission on Terrorist Attacks Upon the United States, *The 9/11 Commission Report: Final Report of the National Commission on Terrorist Attacks Upon the United States* (Washington D.C.: U.S. Government Printing Office, 2004), 14.

[33] *Kamikaze* pilots were named for the "divine winds" that saved Japan in the thirteenth century from Genghis Khan's invasion by capsizing his transport ships before they could reach Japanese soil.

[34] Edwin M. Nakasone, *The Nisei Soldier: Historical Essays on World War II and the Korean War* (White Bear Lake: J-Press, 1999), 75.

[35] Ibid.

[36] Ibid.

[37] Ibid.

[38] Ibid., 76.

[39] Ibid.

[40] Ibid.

[41] Dower, 232.

[42] Ibid.

[43] Nasra Hassan, "An Arsenal of Believers: Talking to the 'Human Bombs,'" *The New Yorker*, November 19, 2001, 40.

[44] In Islam, it is a sin to commit suicide; hence the preferred Islamist term for a suicide bombing is a "sacred explosion." See Hassan, 37; also see *Quran 4:29*, E.H. Palmer, trans, *The Quran* (London: Oxford University Press, 1960), 69; as well as the University of Southern California-MSA Compendium of Muslim Texts, *Hadith* (*Bukhari*) *2:445*, http://www.usc.edu/dept/MSA/fundamentals/hadithsunnah/bukhari/023.sbt.html#002.023.445 (accessed February 24, 2008).

[45] Hassan, 37.

[46] Ibid.

[47] Benedict, 36.

[48] Meirion and Susie Harries, *Soldiers of the Sun: The Rise and Fall of the Imperial Japanese Army* (New York: Random House, 1991), 348.

[49] Ibid., 323.

[50] Ibid., 351.

[51] Ami Pedahzur, *Suicide Terrorism* (Malden: Polity Press, 2005), 156.

[52] Dower, 79.

[53] Ibid., 243.

[54] Ibid.

[55] Ibid.

[56] Ozzie St. George, "Beer Bounty for Japs," *Yank: The Army* Weekly, May 18, 1945.

[57] George W. Bush, "Islam is Peace," *Office of the Press Secretary*, September 17, 2001, http://www.whitehouse.gov/news/releases/2001/09/20010917-11.html (accessed February 14, 2008).

[58] Saar, 51.

[59] Joseph D. Harrington, *Yankee Samurai: The Secret Role of Nisei in America's Pacific Victory* (Detroit: Pettigrew Enterprises, Inc., 1979), 16.

[60] Stone, 4.

[61] As per author's personal knowledge from being trained as an Arabic linguist at the Defense Language Institute Foreign Language Center at Monterrey, California in 1992.

[62] Ibid.

[63] Hanson W. Baldwin, "This is the Army We Have to Defeat; a Picture of the Japanese Soldier and the Organization of Which He is the Core," *New York Times*, July 29, 1945.

[64] Ibid.

[65] Clear, 124.

[66] A full combat pack weighed approximately forty pounds.

[67] U.S. Army Field Manual 3-21.5 (*Drill and Ceremonies*) defines double-time as to march in the cadence of 180 steps per minute with a 30-inch step; the equivalent of running.

[68] Clear, 128.

[69] Ibid.

[70] Benedict, 129.

[71] John L. Esposito, *Islam: The Straight Path* (New York: Oxford University Press, 1991), 5.

[72] William L. Cleveland, *A History of the Middle East* (Boulder: Westview Press, 1994), 6.

[73] Esposito, 15.

[74] Majid Khadduri, *War and Peace in the Law of Islam* (London: The John Hopkins Press, 1955), 59.

[75] Esposito, 35.

[76] J.J. Saunders, *A History of Medieval Islam* (New York: Routledge, 1993), 195.

[77] Fawaz A. Gerges, *Journey of the Jihadist: Inside Muslim Militancy* (Orlando: Harcourt, Inc., 2007), 14.

[78] Ibid.

[79] Joyce M. Davis, *Martyrs: Innocence, Vengeance, and Despair in the Middle East* (New York: Palgrave McMillian, 2003), 7-8.

[80] Ibid. "Kalashnikov" is a nickname for the AK-47 assault rifle, originally designed by Mikhail Kalashnikov.

[81] Gerges, 10.

[82] Joint Military Intelligence College, *Global War on Terrorism: Analyzing the Strategic Threat* (Washington D.C.: Joint Military Intelligence College Press, 2004), 61.

[83] Davis, 100.

[84] Ibid., 148.

[85] Joint Military Intelligence College, 60.

Chapter Three

[1] Earl L. Edwards, Captain, U.S. Army, "Inspection of 'Byron Hot Springs'," April 22, 1942; Record Group 389, Records of the Provost Marshal General; POW Operations Division, Operations Branch, Classified Decimal File 1942-1945, NARA, College Park, MD, 4.

[2] Stansbury F. Haydon, *A History of the Military Intelligence Division, 7 December 1941 – 2 September 1945*, Report no. 725 (Washington D.C.: U.S. Army Center of Military History, 1946), 99.

[3] Van Cleve, 1.

[4] Haydon, 100.

[5] Van Cleve, 2.

[6] U.S. Navy, "Office of Naval Intelligence," in *United States Naval Administration in World War II*, (Washington D.C.: U.S. Naval Historical Center), 873.

[7] For further information on Fort Hunt see Steven Kleinman's "The History of MIS-Y: U.S. Strategic Interrogation During World War II" located at http://handle.dtic.mil/100.2/ADA447589 (accessed February 24, 2008).

[8] Van Cleve, 83.

[9] Edwards, 3.

[10] Ibid., 4.

[11] Van Cleve, 82.

[12] Carol A. Jensen, *Images of America: Byron Hot Springs* (San Francisco: Arcadia Publishing, 2006), 7. For further information concerning the history of the Byron Hot Springs Resort, see the Byron Hot Springs Resort and Spa website at: http://www.byronhotsprings.com/home.html (accessed March 30, 2008).

[13] Ibid., 9.

[14] Ibid., 51.

[15] Edwards, 2.

[16] Due to the classified nature of the JIC, no photographs were allowed to be taken of the facility. Due to this prohibition, there are very few photographs of the hotel during its actual use as a JIC. This photograph was taken in 2007.

[17] Allen W. Gullion, Major General, U.S. Army, "Technical Apparatus for the Second Interrogation Center," April 27, 1942; Record Group 389, Records of the Provost Marshal General; POW Operations Division, Operations Branch, Classified Decimal File 1942-1945, NARA, College Park, MD.

[18] Van Cleve, 44.

[19] Ibid., 82.

[20] Rhodes F. Arnold, Colonel, U.S. Army, "Byron Hot Springs Project," September 6, 1942; Record Group 389, Records of the Provost Marshal General; POW Operations Division, Operations Branch, Classified Decimal File 1942-1945, NARA, College Park, MD, 2.

[21] Ibid., 2.

[22] Ibid., 3.

[23] Van Cleve, 56.

[24] Ibid., 4.

[25] The "M" in "M" room was an abbreviation for "Monitoring."

[26] Van Cleve, 48.

[27] Arnold, 1.

[28] Ibid., 4.

[29] Ibid., 5.

[30] Edwards, 4.

[31] Van Cleve, 74.

[32] H. B. Lewis, Brigadier General, U.S. Army, "Mailing Address for 'Byron Hot Springs', California," August 29, 1942; Record Group 389, Records of the Provost Marshal General; POW Operations Division, Operations Branch, Classified Decimal File 1942-1945, NARA, College Park, MD. In the same fashion, Fort Hunt was referred to as P.O. Box 1142.

[33] Adjutant General, U.S. Army, "Joint Interrogation Centers," May 16, 1942; Record Group 389, Records of the Provost Marshal General; POW Operations Division, Operations Branch, Classified Decimal File 1942-1945, NARA, College Park, MD.

[34] During WWII the words "post" and "camp" were loosely interchangeable in Army jargon.

[35] Van Cleve, 10-11.

[36] Haydon, 101.

[37] Ibid., 11.

[38] B. M. Bryan, Colonel, U.S. Army, "Issuance of Order," July 9, 1942; Record Group 389, Records of the Provost Marshal General; POW Operations Division, Operations Branch, Classified Decimal File 1942-1945, NARA, College Park, MD. COL Kent had also been in charge of the Fort Hunt (P.O. Box 1142) JIC from July 1, 1942, to October 21, 1942, prior to his transfer to the Camp Tracy (P.O. Box 651) JIC.

[39] John Weckerling, Colonel, U.S. Army, "Relief of Post Commander, Fort Hunt, Virginia," March 3, 1943; Record Group 389, Records of the Provost Marshal General; POW Operations Division, Operations Branch, Classified Decimal File 1942-1945, NARA, College Park, MD.

[40] Weckerling, "3rd Indorsement to Relief of Post Commander, Fort Hunt, Virginia," March 13, 1943; Record Group 389, Records of the Provost Marshal General; POW Operations Division, Operations Branch, Classified Decimal File 1942-1945, NARA, College Park, MD.

[41] Van Cleve, 14.

Chapter Four

[1] As quoted in *The Observer* (London), 1952.

[2] In July 1945, Camp Tracy was shut down and all personnel and operations were transferred to Fort Hunt, Virginia.

[3] Van Cleve, 87-88.

[4] "Office of Naval Intelligence," 874.

[5] Ibid., 875

[6] Ibid.

[7] Ibid.

[8] Louis A. Nipkow, Second Lieutenant, U.S. Army, interrogator at Camp Tracy during WWII; telephone interview with author, Washington D.C., January 30, 2008.

[9] Scott Clark, "Guide to the William P. Woodard Papers 1896-1974," *Northwest Digital Archives*, http://nwda-db.wsulibs.wsu.edu/findaid/arki/80444/xv82095 (accessed April 24, 2008).

[10] *Tracy Naval Unit Daily Log Book*, August 1, 1943; Record Group 38, Records of the Navy; Special Activities Branch (OP-16-Z), Navy Unit, Tracy, California, NARA, College Park, MD.

[11] William P. Woodard, Lieutenant, U.S. Navy, "Tentative Schedule," January 12, 1943; Record Group 38, Records of the Navy; Special Activities Branch (OP-16-Z), Navy Unit, Tracy, California, NARA, College Park, MD.

[12] David W. Swift Jr., ed., *Ninety Li A Day* (Taipei: The Orient Cultural Service, 1975), 1.

[13] Ibid., 58.

[14] Ibid., 268.

[15] Ibid., 281.

[16] Nipkow.

[17] Richard P. Kleeman, Second Lieutenant, U.S. Army, interrogator at Camp Tracy during WWII; interview by Fort Hunt Oral History Program, Washington D.C., September 13, 2007. Nisei are people of Japanese ancestry but are the first generation born abroad from Japan.

[18] Ben I. Yamamoto, "The Adventures of an MIS Marine," in *Japanese Eyes, American Heart: Personal Reflections of Hawaii's World War II Nisei Soldiers* (Honolulu: University of Hawai'i Press, 1998), 178. The MISLS moved from Camp Savage to Fort Snelling, Minnesota in 1944 and remained there for the duration of the war.

[19] David M. Hays, "Words at War: The Sensei of the US Navy Japanese Language School at the University of Colorado, 1942-1946," *Discover Nikkei: Japanese Migrants and their Descendents*, April 9, 2008, http://www.discovernikkei.org/forum/en/node/ 2360 (accessed April 28, 2008). Issei are Japanese persons who have emigrated from Japan. Issei are the parents of the Nisei. The U.S. Navy Japanese Language School originally was located at the University of California at Berkeley, California, but was forced to relocate to the University of Colorado in 1941 due to U.S. Executive Order 9066 which established California as an exclusionary zone against those with "foreign enemy ancestry."

[20] For further information on the U.S. Army and U.S. Navy Japanese language programs during WWII see Stone, 37-81.

[21] Nipkow.

[22] Charles Y. Banfill, Brigadier General, U.S. Army, "Brief of Pertinent Facts and Data Concerning the Military Intelligence Training Center, Camp Ritchie, Maryland," June 3, 1944; Record Group 165, Records of the War Department General and Special Staffs; Training Records of the MITC, NARA, College Park, MD, 2.

[23] Henry R. Winkler, Ensign U.S. Navy, interrogator at Camp Tracy during WWII; letter to author, April 4, 2008; Lionel Casson, Ensign U.S. Navy, interrogator at Camp Tracy during WWII; telephone interview with author, Washington D.C., April 25, 2008.

[24] Woodard.

[25] Ulrich Straus, *The Anguish of Surrender: Japanese POWs of World War II* (Seattle: University of Washington Press, 2003), 17.

[26] Ibid., 48.

[27] Ibid.

[28] Ibid.

[29] Ibid., 49.

[30] Ibid., 172.

[31] See Appendix A for an example of a strategic-level questionnaire sent to Camp Tracy for use during interrogations of Japanese POWs.

[32] Haydon, 102.

[33] Ibid.

[34] Ferris, 1.

[35] Yamamoto, 179.

[36] Haydon, 105.

[37] Arnold Krammer, "Japanese Prisoners of War in America," *The Pacific Historical Review* 52, no. 1 (February 1983): 76; Ferris, 1-2.

[38] Van Cleve, 87-88; Ferris, 1.

[39] Homer M. Groninger, Major General, U.S. Army, "Disposition of Japanese Prisoners of War at Camp Stoneman," July 20, 1945, Record Group 389, Records of the Provost Marshal General; Prisoner of War Operations Div, Operations Branch, Classified Decimal File 1942-45, NARA, College Park, MD, 1.

[40] Zenas R. Bliss, Lieutenant Colonel, U.S. Army, "Processing and Screening Facilities for Prisoners of War as related to activities of P. O. Box 651, Tracy, California," February 27, 1945, Record Group 165, Records of the War Department General and Special Staffs; Office of the Director of Intelligence (G-2), Subordinate Office and Branches, Captured Personnel and Material Branch, Enemy POW Interrogation File (MIS-Y) 1943-45; Country File Japan – Reports Interrogation Extracts Vol 11 to Reports Distribution, NARA, College Park, MD, 4.

[41] Haydon, 103.

[42] Harry T. Gherardi, Commander, U.S. Navy, "Interrogation of Prisoners," Record Group 38, Records of the Navy; Special Activities Branch (OP-16-Z), Navy Unit, Tracy, California, NARA, College Park, MD, 1.

[43] Ibid.

[44] "Prisoners of War as a Source of Information," Record Group 38, Records of the Navy; Special Activities Branch (OP-16-Z), Navy Unit, Tracy, California, NARA, College Park, MD, 2.

[45] Gherardi, 3.

[46] Ibid., 1.

[47] Ibid.

[48] Van Cleve, 38.

[49] Gherardi, 2.

[50] Van Cleve, 39.

[51] Haydon, 104.

[52] "Prisoners of War as a Source of Information," 5.

[53] Gherardi, 2.

[54] "Prisoners of War as a Source of Information," 5.

[55] The Nisei interrogators were all members of the U.S. military, though the majority of them were Enlisted instead of Officers.

[56] Nipkow.

[57] Ibid.

[58] Gherardi, 2.

[59] Nipkow.

[60] "Prisoners of War as a Source of Information," 5.

[61] As per U.S. Army Field Manual 34-52 (*Intelligence Interrogation*), dated 28 September 1992, to "break" a POW is to overcome his natural reluctance to answer questions. POWs are considered "broken" when they begin to answer questions freely without any apparent hesitation or mental reservation. And continue to cooperate with the questioning. The new U.S. Army Field Manual 2-22.3 (*Human Intelligence Collector Operations*), dated 6 September 2006, changes the terminology from "breaking" a POW, to gaining a POW's "cooperation."

[62] Gherardi, 2.

[63] Straus, 130; personal research notes of Ulrich Straus on Ishii Shuji, sent to author, November 8, 2007.

[64] Gherardi, 2.

[65] John A. Burden, Captain, U.S. Army, "Interrogation of Japanese Prisoners in the Southwest Pacific," July 22, 1943; Record Group 389, Records of the Provost Marshal General; Enemy POW Information Bureau, Reporting Branch, Subject File 1942-1946, NARA, College Park, MD, 6.

[66] Nipkow; Straus, 120.

[67] George E. Mendenhall, Ensign U.S. Navy, interrogator at Camp Tracy during WWII; letter to author, April 3, 2008.

[68] Straus, 130-131; also as per author's intensive research at the U.S. National Archives.

[69] Interrogators at Camp Tracy used fake names to protect their identities and the identities of their families. Mr. "Coleman" was in fact U.S. Navy Agent H. Colton. For a complete list of names and aliases of Camp Tracy interrogators see: *PW Interrogation Record*, June 14, 1944; Record Group 165, General and Special Staffs, G-2; Captured Personnel and Materiel Branch, Enemy POW Interrogation File (MIS-Y) 1943-1945, NARA, College Park, MD.

[70] Straus, 131; personal research notes of Ulrich Straus on Nakajima Yoshio, sent to author, November 8, 2007.

[71] *Interrogation Logbook.*

[72] "Prisoners of War as a Source of Intelligence," 2.

[73] Van Cleve, 38.

[74] Hayden, 104.

[75] Van Cleve, 67.

[76] "Prisoners of War as a Source of Information," 9.

[77] Gherardi, 3.

[78] Van Cleve, 41.

[79] Ibid.

[80] Ibid., 42.

[81] Ibid.

[82] "Prisoners of War as a Source of Information," 10.

[83] Ibid., 11; Burden, 7.

[84] Gherardi, 2.

[85] "Prisoners of War as a Source of Information," 11.

[86] Van Cleve, 46-47.

[87] See Appendix B for the Camp Tracy approved structure and format for Interrogation Reports.

[88] During WWII another common way to abbreviate Prisoner of War was "P/W" or "Ps/W" to indicate Prisoners of War.

[89] Van Cleve, 46.

[90] Gherardi, 3.

[91] Zenas R. Bliss, Lieutenant Colonel, U.S. Army, "Nisei Personnel," May 30, 1945; Record Group 165, General and Special Staffs, G-2;

Captured Personnel and Materiel Branch, Enemy POW Interrogation File (MIS-Y) 1943-1945, NARA, College Park, MD, 1; Straus, 137.

[92] "The Military Intelligence Service Language School," Record Group 165, Records of the War Department General and Special Staffs, Correspondence and Reports Relating to the Operation of Language Schools, 1943-1949, NARA, College Park, MD, 7.

[93] Straus, 137.

[94] See Appendix C for the complete interrogation packet on Eikichi Saito covering his initial screening and interrogation in the Pacific Theater to his transfer and interrogation at Camp Tracy.

Chapter Five

[1] Center for the Study of Intelligence, "George Washington, 1789-97," *Central Intelligence Agency*, March 19, 2007, https://www.cia.gov/library/center-for-the-study-of-intelligence/csi-publications/books-and-monographs/our-first-line-of-defense-presidential-reflections-on-us-intelligence/washington.html (accessed May 30, 2008).

[2] "Office of Naval Intelligence," 874.

[3] Ibid., 875.

[4] Van Cleve, 38.

Epilogue

[1] Krammer, 89; the only exceptions were 24 Japanese POWs who had died during their captivity and were buried in the United States. Even then, by 1954, 17 of the 24 POWs had been exhumed and the remains returned to Japan.

Appendix A

[1] "Propaganda and Morale Questionnaire," Record Group 389, Records of the Provost Marshal General; POW Operations Division, Operations Branch, Classified Decimal File 1942-1945, NARA, College Park, MD, 1-8. This questionnaire is recreated here as it appeared in the archives; no corrections have been made from the original.

[2] Note: "Tab B" is not included in this Appendix.

Appendix B

[1] "Outline for Interrogations," Record Group 165, Records of the War Department General and Special Staffs; Office of the Director of Intelligence (G-2), Subordinate Office and Branches, Captured Personnel and Material Branch, Enemy POW Interrogation File (MIS-Y) 1943-45; Country File Japan – Reports Interrogation Extracts Vol 11 to Reports Distribution, NARA, College Park, MD, 1-8. This document is recreated here as it appeared in the archives; no corrections have been made from the original.

Appendix C

[1] This Appendix is compiled from declassified documents found within two Record Groups: Record Group 165, Records of the War Department General and Special Staffs; Office of the Director of Intelligence (G-2), Subordinate Office and Branches, Captured Personnel and Material Branch, Enemy POW Interrogation File (MIS-Y) 1943-45, NARA, College Park, MD; and Record Group 38, Records of the Navy; Special Activities Branch (OP-16-Z), Navy Unit, Tracy, California, NARA, College Park, MD.

References

ABC News.com. "Translation of Sept. 11 Hijacker Mohamed Atta's Suicide Note: Part Two." *ABC News*, September 28, 2001. http://abcnews.go.com/International/Story?id=79167&page=2 (accessed February 24, 2008).

Adams, Matthew. Technical Sergeant-5 U.S. Army, interrogator at Camp Tracy during WWII. Interview by author, Washington, D.C., November 7, 2007.

Associated Press. "Secret Center at Byron Hot Springs for Quizzing Japs, Germans Told." *Stockton Record*, July 10, 1947.

Baldwin, Hanson W. "This is the Army We Have to Defeat; a Picture of the Japanese Soldier and the Organization of Which He is the Core." *New York Times*, July 29, 1945.

BBC. "Iraq Jail Attack Kills 22 Inmates." *BBC News*, April 20, 2004. http://news.bbc.co.uk/2/hi/ middle_east/3643151.stm (accessed February 11, 2008).

Benedict, Ruth. *The Chrysanthemum and the Sword: Patterns of Japanese Culture*. Rutland: Charles E. Tuttle Company, 1954.

Bush, George W. "Islam is Peace." *Office of the Press Secretary*,

September 17, 2001. http://www.whitehouse.gov/news/
releases/2001/09/20010917-11.html (accessed February 14,
2008).

_____. "President Discusses Creation of Military Commissions to Try
Suspected Terrorists," *Office of the Press Secretary*, Washington,
DC, September 6, 2006, http://www.whitehouse.gov/
news/releases/2006/09/print/20060906-3.html (accessed
November 4, 2008).

Casson, Lionel. Ensign U.S. Navy, interrogator at Camp Tracy during
WWII. Interview by author, Washington, D.C., April 25, 2008.

Center for the Study of Intelligence. "George Washington, 1789-97."
Central Intelligence Agency, March 19, 2007.
https://www.cia.gov/library/center-for-the-study-of-
intelligence/csi-publications/books-and-monographs/our-first-
line-of-defense-presidential-reflections-on-us-
intelligence/washington.html (accessed May 30, 2008).

Christopher, Robert C. *The Japanese Mind: The Goliath Explained*. New
York: Linden Press, 1983.

Clear, Warren J. "Close Up of the Jap Fighting Man." *Reader's Digest*
41, November 1942, 124-130.

Cleveland, William L. *A History of the Middle East*. Boulder: Westview
Press, 1994.

Corbin, Jane. *Al-Qaeda: In Search of the Terror Network that Threatens
the World*. New York: Thunder's Mouth Press / Nation Books,
2003.

Crost, Lyn. *Honor by Fire: Japanese Americans at War in Europe and the
Pacific*. Novato: Presidio Press, 1994.

Davis, Joyce M. *Martyrs: Innocence, Vengeance, and Despair in the
Middle East*. New York: Palgrave McMillian, 2003.

Dower, John W. *Embracing Defeat: Japan in the Wake of World War II*.
New York: W. W. Norton & Company, 1999.

_____. *War Without Mercy: Race & Power in the Pacific War*. New
York: Pantheon Books, 1986.

Dvorak, Petula. "Fort Hunt's Quiet Men Break Silence on WWII: Interrogator Fought 'Battle of Wits'." *The Washington Post*, October 6, 2007, http://www.washingtonpost.com/wp-dyn/content/article/2007/ 10/05/AR2007100502492.html (accessed November 4, 2008).

Esposito, John L. *Islam: The Straight Path*. New York: Oxford University Press, 1991.

Foxx, A.G. "Your Enemy: The Jap." *Infantry Journal* 56 (March 1945): 24-25.

Gerges, Fawaz A. *Journey of the Jihadist: Inside Muslim Militancy*. Orlando: Harcourt, Inc., 2007.

Hagee, Chuck. "Talk Was Their Weapon—Silence Their Legacy: Their Recognition Waved in the Morning Sun at Exactly 11:42." *Arlington Connection*, October 9, 2008, http://www.connectionnewspapers.com/ article.asp?article= 309498&paper=60&cat=104 (accessed November 4, 2008).

Harries, Meirion and Susie Harries. *Soldiers of the Sun: The Rise and Fall of the Imperial Japanese Army*. New York: Random House, 1991.

Harrington, Joseph D. *Yankee Samurai: The Secret Role of Nisei in America's Pacific Victory*. Detroit: Pettigrew Enterprises, Inc., 1979.

Hassan, Nasra. "An Arsenal of Believers: Talking to the 'Human Bombs'." *The New Yorker*, November 19, 2001, 34-40.

Hawaii Nikkei History Editorial Board. *Japanese Eyes, American Heart: Personal Reflections of Hawaii's World War II Nisei Soldiers*. Honolulu: University of Hawai'i Press, 1998.

Haydon, F. Stansbury. *A History of the Military Intelligence Division, 7 December 1941 – 2 September 1945*. Report no. 725. Washington D.C.: U.S. Army Center of Military History, 1946.

Hays, David M. "Words at War: The Sensei of the US Navy Japanese Language School at the University of Colorado, 1942-1946." *Discover Nikkei: Japanese Migrants and their Descendents*, April 9, 2008. http://www.discovernikkei.org/forum/en/node/ 2360 (accessed April 28, 2008).

Hoare, Oliver, ed. *Camp 020: MI5 and the Nazi Spies*. Bath: Bath Press Ltd., 2000.

"How War Prisoners Behave." *Science Digest* 15, no. 4 (April 1944): 29-30.

Jensen, Carol A. *Images of America: Byron Hot Springs*. San Francisco: Arcadia Publishing, 2006.

Joint Military Intelligence College. *Global War on Terrorism: Analyzing the Strategic Threat*. Washington D.C.: Joint Military Intelligence College Press, 2004.

Khadduri, Majid. *War and Peace in the Law of Islam*. London: The John Hopkins Press, 1955.

Kleeman, Richard. Second Lieutenant U.S. Army, interrogator at Camp Tracy during WWII. Interview by Fort Hunt Oral History Program, Washington D.C., September 13, 2007.

Kleinman, Steven M. "The History of MIS-Y: U.S. Strategic Interrogation in World War II." Master's thesis, Joint Military Intelligence College, 2002.

Krammer, Arnold. "Japanese Prisoners of War in America." *The Pacific Historical Review* 52, no. 1 (February 1983): 67-91.

Lemyre, Rick. "In the Shadows of Camp Tracy." *Brentwood Press.com*, March 7, 2008. http://www.brentwoodpress.com/article.cfm?articleID=18972 (accessed March 7, 2008).

Littlewood, Ian. *The Idea of Japan: Western Images, Western Myths*. Chicago: Ivan R. Dee, Inc., 1996.

Lory, Hillis. *Japan's Military Masters: The Army in Japanese Life*. New York: Viking Press, 1943.

McKelvey, Tara. *Monstering: Inside America's Policy of Secret Interrogations and Torture in the Terror War*. New York: Carroll & Graf Publishers, 2007.

McNaughton, James C. *Nisei Linguists: Japanese Americans in the Military Intelligence Service during World War II*. Washington, D.C.: Department of the Army, 2006.

Mendenhall, George. Ensign U.S. Navy, interrogator at Camp Tracy during WWII. Interview by author, Washington D.C., March 31, 2008.

Moody, Sidney C. Jr. *War Against Japan.* Novato: Presidio Press, 1994.

Moore, Bob and Kent Fedorowich. *The British Empire and its Italian Prisoners of War, 1940-1947.* New York: Palgrave, 2002.

Moore, John Hammond. "Getting Fritz to Talk." *The Virginia Quarterly Review* 54, no. 2 (Spring 1978): 263-281.

Nakasone, Edwin M. *The Nisei Soldier: Historical Essays on World War II and the Korean War.* White Bear Lake: J-Press, 1999.

National Archives and Records Administration. Record Group 38. Records of the Navy; Special Activities Branch (OP-16-Z), Navy Unit, Tracy, California. National Archives and Records Administration, College Park, MD.

_____. Record Group 165. Records of the War Department General and Special Staffs; Office of the Director of Intelligence (G-2), Subordinate Office and Branches, Captured Personnel and Material Branch. National Archives and Records Administration, College Park, MD.

_____. Record Group 389. Provost Marshal General, Executive Division, Technical Information Officer Publicity File, 1942-1945. National Archives and Records Administration, College Park, MD.

National Commission on Terrorist Attacks Upon the United States. *The 9/11 Commission Report: Final Report of the National Commission on Terrorist Attacks Upon the United States.* Washington D.C.: U.S. Government Printing Office, 2004.

Nipkow, Louis. Second Lieutenant U.S. Army, interrogator at Camp Tracy during WWII. Interview by author, Washington, D.C., January 30, 2008.

Office of the Director of National Intelligence. *The National Intelligence Strategy of the United States of America.* Washington, D.C.: 2005. http://www.dni.gov/publications/ NISOctober2005.pdf (accessed November 14, 2007).

Pedahzur, Ami. *Suicide Terrorism*. Malden: Polity Press, 2005.

Saar, Erik and Viveca Novak. *Inside the Wire: A Military Intelligence Soldier's Eyewitness Account of Life at Guantanamo*. New York: The Penguin Press, 2005.

Saunders, J.J. *A History of Medieval Islam*. New York: Routledge, 1993.

Schrijivers, Peter. *The GI War Against Japan: American Soldiers in Asia and the Pacific During World War II*. New York: New York University Press, 2002.

Serrano, Richard A. "Pentagon: Koran Defiled." *Los Angeles Times*, June 4, 2005.

Spector, Ronald H. *Eagle Against the Sun*. New York: Random House, 1985.

Strasser, Steven, ed. *The Abu Ghraib Investigations: The Official Reports of the Independent Panel and the Pentagon on the Shocking Prisoner Abuse in Iraq*. New York: PublicAffairs, 2004.

Straus, Ulrich. *The Anguish of Surrender: Japanese POWs of World War II*. Seattle: University of Washington Press, 2003.

St. George, Ozzie. "Beer Bounty for Japs." *Yank: The Army* Weekly, May 18, 1945.

Stolberg, Sheryl Gay. "Bush Says Interrogation Methods Aren't Torture." *New York Times*, October 6, 2007. http://www.nytimes.com/2007/10/06/U.S./nationalspecial3/06interrogate.html (accessed November 25, 2007).

Stone, James A. "Interrogations of Japanese POWs in WWII: U.S. Response to a Formidable Challenge." Master's thesis, National Defense Intelligence College, 2007.

Swift, David W. Jr., ed. *Ninety Li A Day*. Taipei: The Orient Cultural Service, 1975.

Temple-Raston, Dina. *The Jihad Next Door*. New York: PublicAffairs, 2007.

Toland, John. *The Rising Sun: The Decline and Fall of the Japanese*

Empire, 1936-1945. New York: Random House, 1970.

U.S. Army. Field Manual 2-22.3, *Human Intelligence Collector Operations.* Washington, D.C.: Government Publishing Office, 2006.

U.S. Congress. *Congressional Records.* 110th Congress, 1st session, 2007. S4407.

U.S. Department of Defense. "DoD News Briefing with Deputy Assistant Secretary Stimson and Lt. Gen. Kimmons from the Pentagon." *Office of the Assistant Secretary of Defense (Public Affairs),* September 6, 2006. http://www.defenselink.mil/ transcripts/transcript.aspx?transcriptid=3712 (accessed February 11, 2008).

U.S. Navy. "Office of Naval Intelligence," in *United States Naval Administration in World War II.* Washington D.C.: U.S. Naval Historical Center.

U.S. War Department. *Know Your Enemy: Japan.* DVD. Directed by Frank Capra, originally released August 9, 1945. Kaiserslautern, Germany: Custom Flix, 2005.

Wedeman, Ben. "Shock, Outrage Over Prison Photos." *CNN.com*, May 1, 2004. http://edition.cnn.com/2004/WORLD/meast/04/30/ Iraq.photos/index.html (accessed November 30, 2007).

William P. Woodard Papers. University of Oregon Library, Eugene, OR.

Willis, Donald S. Ensign U.S. Navy, interrogator at Camp Tracy during WWII. Interview by author, Washington, D.C., March 27, 2008.

Winkler, Henry. Ensign U.S. Navy, interrogator at Camp Tracy during WWII. Interview by author, Washington, D.C., March 31, 2008.

Index

About the Author

Alexander D. Corbin is an active-duty Military Intelligence (MI) officer in the U.S. Army. He currently serves as the J2 intelligence advisor to the Ministry of Defense and Aviation in the Kingdom of Saudi Arabia. During his military career of more than 17 years, Major Corbin has served in human intelligence and counterintelligence positions at the tactical, operational, and strategic levels in the Balkans, Egypt, Kuwait, and Iraq. Drawing on his extensive background in U.S. Army MI future-force development, he has written, developed, and published doctrine for the U.S. Army Future Combat Systems' MI organizations as part of the Future Brigade Combat Team. Major Corbin also serves as an adjunct professor at Henley-Putnam University where he teaches intelligence and security-related courses.

Major Corbin holds a master's degree in military studies (intelligence) from the American Military University, and a master's degree in strategic intelligence from the National Defense Intelligence College. He received undergraduate degrees in political science and Middle East studies (Arabic), as well as a certificate in international relations, from the University of Utah in Salt Lake City, Utah.

Major Corbin can be reached at alex.corbin@yahoo.com.